Easy Does It® for Preschool/Primary

by Barbara A. Roseman and Karin L. Johnson

Skill	Ages	Grades
■ fluency	■ 2 through 6	■ PreK through 1

Evidence-Based Practice

- ASHA (1995) promotes use of a hierarchy going from single words to conversation fluently, role-playing social situations to desensitize a patient's reaction to stuttering, and implementing parent and teacher support for carryover of targeted fluency skills.

- Fluent children between four and five years of age can distinguish between fluent and disfluent speech and usually assign a negative label to disfluent speech. Children often reported they wanted to be friends with a child who showed fluent speech. This has clinical implications of not only the rationale that very young children can identify disfluent speech, but also the negative social consequences if a young child does not improve with fluency strategies (Ezrati-Vinacour, Platzky, Yairi, 2001).

- Preschool children who stutter were found to have quicker response times and more fluent speech during a picture description task after a priming sentence was provided versus when no priming sentence was provided (Anderson & Conture, 2004). Use of imitation, carrier phrases, and speech modeling in this book all provide examples of priming as a fluency enhancing measure.

- Young children who stutter showed more difficulty adapting to a new environment, showed greater attention span, and more variability in biological patterns, such as hunger and sleep, in comparison to children who do not stutter. A therapy approach should take these results into account to provide effective fluency intervention (Anderson, Pellowski, Conture, & Kelly, 2003).

- Use of fluent conversational skills, in various social situations relevant to the child, need to be directly addressed in therapy for successful transfer of targeted skills and discharge from speech therapy services (Weiss, 2004).

Easy Does It for Fluency Preschool/Primary incorporates these principles and is also based on expert professional practice.

References

American Speech-Language-Hearing Association (ASHA). (1995). *Guidelines for practice in stuttering treatment.* Retrieved September 9, 2009, from www.asha.org/policy

Anderson, J.D., & Conture, E.G. (2004). Sentence-structure priming in young children who do and do not stutter. *Journal of Speech, Language, and Hearing Research, 47,* 552-571.

Anderson, J.D., Pellowski, M.W., Conture, E.G., & Kelly, E.M. (2003). Temperamental characteristics of young children who stutter. *Journal of Speech, Language, and Hearing Research, 46,* 1221-1233.

Ezrati-Vinacour, R., Platzky, R., & Yairi, E. (2001). The young child's awareness of stuttering-like disfluency. *Journal of Speech, Language, and Hearing Research, 44,* 368-380.

Weiss, A.L. (2004). Why we should consider pragmatics when planning treatment for children who stutter. *Language, Speech, and Hearing Services in Schools, 35,* 34-45.

LinguiSystems®

Copyright © 1998 LinguiSystems, Inc.

All of our products are copyrighted to protect the fine work of our authors. All rights are reserved, including the right to reproduce this work or portions thereof in any form, including copying the entire book to use as another primary source or "master" copy.

LinguiSystems, Inc.
3100 4th Avenue
East Moline, IL 61244
800-776-4332

FAX: 800-577-4555
Email: service@linguisystems.com
Web: linguisystems.com

Printed in the U.S.A.

ISBN 10: 0-7606-0169-0
ISBN 13: 978-0-7606-0169-3

About the Authors

Barbara A. Roseman, M.A., CCC-SLP, is an associate professor at Augustana College in Rock Island, IL. She is also the director of the Augustana College Center for Communicative Disorders. Barbara is the past-president and Fellow of the Illinois Speech and Hearing Association.

Karin L. Johnson, M.A., CCC-SLP, is an associate professor at Augustana College in Rock Island, IL. She is also the director of the speech-language pathology program, the chair of the Department of Speech Communications and Theater Arts, and the chair of the Fine Arts Division at Augustana College.

Barbara and Karin have co-authored numerous publications in the areas of fluency disorders, motor speech disorders, narratives, birth-to-three intervention, and metalinguistics. These long-time LinguiSystems' authors have also written *The Fluency Companion* and *Easy Does It for Fluency-Intermediate*.

Dedication
We dedicate this book to our parents: Edna R. Allen and the late Milton A. Allen and Blenda L. and H. Milton Lundahl for their faith in us.

Acknowledgment
Appreciation to Laura, Sarah, Kathy, Cindy, and Bob for their enthusiastic support and encouragement.

Table of Contents

Introduction 5

Step 1: Experiencing Easy Speech 9

Step 2: Establishing Easy Speech 11

Step 3: Desensitizing to Fluency Disrupters 49

Step 4: Transferring Fluency 66

Step 5: Maintaining Fluency 96

Combined Phonological and Fluency Therapy 98

Home and Daycare/Preschool Letters 99

Sample Lesson Plans 111

Introduction

Easy Does It for Fluency - Preschool/Primary is an individualized, systematic therapy program for children ages two through six with stuttering disorders. This program is systematically organized, but is not meant to be a "cookbook." Carefully look at the progression of activities and tailor them to meet the needs of each child.

We have attempted to anticipate and address possible problems that may arise when you are working with a child. In addition, we have provided specific activities for parents/caregivers and daycare/preschool teachers.

Rationale

Easy Does It for Fluency - Preschool/Primary is based on the principle that much learning takes place through modeling. Because easy speech can be learned the same way, the use of modeling is an inherent component of this program. Goals and objectives are set up in a hierarchy to enhance shaping and generalization of the easy speech.

This therapy program is an integrated approach that combines the flexibility of stuttering modification with the structure of fluency shaping. It is systematically organized based on developmental norms, interest level, and author experience.

This program addresses three components usually theorized as potential causes of stuttering:

1. **Motor**
   This is addressed by modeling easy speech using slightly exaggerated inflection patterns and a slow speaking rate (usually about 90 to 110 words per minute). As the program progresses, you will model normal inflection patterns and a speaking rate that matches a rate conducive to fluency for the child. Typically, that rate is about 110 to 130 words per minute, a slower rate than is usually used by an adult. Easy onsets, light contacts, and continuous phonation will also be modeled, but not directly taught.

2. **Linguistic**
   This component focuses on length of utterance. As you introduce different tasks, the child produces one-word utterances. The child's utterance length eventually increases to sentences and then to conversation. Initially, the child will respond by imitating, and then progress to use of stereotyped and carrier sentences. The complexity of the linguistic task increases with question-and-answer tasks. Finally, the child engages in conversation.

   Language appropriate for young children is used throughout this program. Activities help to develop vocabulary and syntax as well as to introduce words that are often difficult for the child who is stuttering (e.g., I, what). In addition, transfer tasks are organized around pragmatic functions of informing, controlling, ritualizing, expressing feelings, and imagining.

3. Psychosocial

This is addressed by incorporating work on attitudes. Since the people with whom a child has contact may impact therapy, activities involve the people most important in the life of a young child. Similarly, since fluency can be affected by disruptions, a number of fluency disrupters are introduced to desensitize the child to their influence.

Basic Principles

Easy Does It for Fluency - Preschool/Primary is divided into five steps for the child to work through to reach his goal of fluent speech.

Step 1: Experiencing Easy Speech
The child experiences fluency through the use of slow, easy speech. During the activities in this section, model a slower speaking rate (120-130 syllables per minute or 90 to 110 words per minute). Also use appropriate inflection, stress, and pausing patterns.

Step 2: Establishing Easy Speech
The child establishes fluency through use of easy speech. We have found that modeling slightly exaggerated inflection patterns may be needed at the onset of this step. Continue modeling a slower speaking rate.

Step 3: Desensitizing to Fluency Disrupters
The child maintains use of easy speech while tolerating pressures which may cause a disintegration of fluency.

Step 4: Transferring Fluency
The child transfers easy speech from structured activities to real-life speaking situations.

Step 5: Maintaining Fluency
The child maintains fluency while decreasing the frequency of direct therapy contacts.

This program progresses in order from Step 1 through Step 5, but there is some overlap in completion. For example, work on transferring fluency begins in a subtle manner during Step 2, and work on desensitization continues from Step 3 throughout Step 4.

It's difficult to determine a child's success rate in completion of each step, but experience has revealed that most children are able to complete Step 1 within one or two sessions. Because most children are able to experience fluency using the activities in this step, it's helpful to review these activities at the beginning of subsequent sessions. It's also helpful to use the activities to reestablish fluency when a child is having problems. Many children are able to complete Step 2 more quickly than Steps 3, 4, and 5.

When beginning this program, daily therapy is ideal. If daily therapy is not possible, schedule therapy for at least two half-hour sessions per week. Individual therapy sessions are recommended throughout the program, with some group sessions when working on Steps 3 and 4.

Lesson Plans

Sample lesson plans are included to demonstrate how a number of objectives may be targeted within one session (pages 111-117). It's important to realize that the number of activities targeted within any objective as well as the number of different objectives targeted within any session will vary significantly depending on each child. For example, one child might need to complete many activities targeting the same objective before mastery is achieved, while another may need to complete only one or two activities.

We suggest that you begin and end sessions with an activity that the child can accomplish fluently.

Assessing Progress

Easy Does It for Fluency - Preschool/Primary is not a step-by-step approach, but rather a systematic therapy program individualized for each child. Therefore, no criteria for completion have been established. Instead, allow the child to experience a high degree of fluency before moving to the next objective.

In general, a child is ready for dismissal after:

- demonstrating less than two part-word repetitions per 100 words and no struggle behaviors
- demonstrating less than one prolongation per 100 words and no struggle behaviors
- you and the child's family feel that the child's fluency is appropriate for his age

Integration of Phonological Therapy

Recent research has indicated that a large number of children with disfluencies also demonstrate phonological deficits. Since it's possible to address both disorders simultaneously, suggestions on how to do so are included (page 98).

Indirect vs. Direct Therapy

Indirect
When working with many young children, you do not need to identify a child's stuttering behavior. Instead, an indirect program is sufficient. Modeling easy speech and encouraging the child to speak the same way often results in fluent speech for the child.

When therapy is indirect, direct reinforcement is not needed, nor is it recommended. Every effort should be made to prevent calling attention to the child's speech. Use of direct reinforcement, such as saying "good talking," often defeats the purpose of indirect therapy. It's recommended that indirect reinforcement be used with comments like "That was fun," or "We played that game well."

Direct

Some children may benefit from a more direct approach. These children are often more severely involved. They are usually aware of their problems with fluency and need direct suggestions on how to change their speech. If needed, introduce the terms "hard talking" and "easy talking." Tell the child that there are two ways to talk, "a hard, pushing" way and an "easy" way. Model the easy way and encourage the child to "talk in the easy way." The puppet EZ (Materials Book, page 7) may help introduce the concept in a concrete way. Use both concrete and verbal reinforcement in Step 2, Establishing Fluency.

Involvement of Support Providers

Before beginning therapy, talk to the child's parents/caregivers about the therapy program. Explain the program, its objectives, and how it progresses from easy, structured tasks to harder, conversational tasks. Explain how the length and complexity of responses is carefully controlled and that activities are designed to meet the interest level and the language level of the child. Stress the importance of family involvement throughout the program. Talk about the need for family members to participate in sessions and to implement suggestions at home.

Make sure to communicate with parents/caregivers routinely. Letters are included (pages 99-110) for you to send home at the onset of each step. Occasionally arrange a face-to-face meeting so you can answer questions or model activities to practice at home.

If the child is in a daycare or preschool setting, ask the parents/caregivers to sign a release (Materials Book, page 96) so you may communicate with the personnel in those settings. Once you have obtained the release, talk to daycare/school personnel at the onset of therapy. Explain the program and its objectives, just as you described it to the child's parents/caregivers. Make sure to communicate routinely to answer questions and receive input. Invite personnel to observe and/or participate in therapy sessions. Letters are also included in the Therapy Manual (pages 99-110) for you to send to daycare/preschool personnel at the onset of each step.

We hope you find this program to be as helpful in planning your therapy as we have. Remember to use it as a guide when planning an individualized therapy program for each child. Feel free to add your own creative touches!

Barbara and Karin

Step 1: Experiencing Easy Speech

> **Goal:** The child will experience easy speech.

A child needs to experience easy speech in order to establish it. One way to help the child experience easy speech is to have him join you in singing familiar songs, reciting nursery rhymes, and doing finger plays.

First, introduce singing, as it is easier than talking. When the child has experienced fluency while singing, follow with nursery rhymes. This task is more complex because the child will be talking. Finally, introduce finger plays. These will be the most difficult because they involve talking while doing actions.

Because the child has a greater chance for success when doing activities with another person, do all activities in unison. During these activities, use a slow rate (90-110 words per minute) with very easy speech.

It should not take more than one or two sessions to complete this objective. To help the child continue to experience easy speech, use songs, nursery rhymes, and finger plays at the beginning of subsequent sessions.

Suggestions for Support Providers

Encourage parents/caregivers and daycare/preschool personnel to sing, recite rhymes, and do finger plays for 5 to 10 minutes per day. These activities are also a good way to calm a child who is excited, upset, or just having a bad day.

Send Home Letter #1 (page 99) and Daycare/Preschool Letter #1 (page 100). These letters talk about the first step in the program, Experiencing Easy Speech. They also include a list of suggested songs, nursery rhymes, and finger plays (page 101). Use of slow, easy speech and movements during the activities is encouraged.

> **Objective:** The child will experience slow, easy speech while singing familiar songs, reciting nursery rhymes, and talking while doing finger plays (page 101).

Procedure

Invite the child to join you in singing familiar songs, reciting nursery rhymes, and talking while doing finger plays. Do these activities in unison with the child and use slow, easy speech.

What if the child doesn't know the song, rhyme, or finger play? Tell the child that you will do the activity twice while he listens. Then, the third time, ask the child to join in. By that time, the child will probably be able to recite the key words or phrases.

Step 1, *continued*

What if the child won't join in? Try a different song, rhyme, or finger play to see if the child will join you. Later, talk to the parent or daycare/preschool personnel (if you have written permission from the parent) to get other suggestions for songs the child might know. If the child continues to be unresponsive, skip this step and go on to Step 2. Encourage the parent and any caregivers to present the songs, rhymes, and finger plays in their environments in an attempt to get the child to join in.

Activity 1

Directions: Say, "I know how to sing 'Old MacDonald.' Let's sing it together." Then, sing other familiar children's songs using slow, easy speech. Have the child sing with you. Some suggested songs are:

- Old MacDonald
- Mary Had a Little Lamb
- Happy Birthday
- Here We Go 'Round the Mulberry Bush
- London Bridge
- Ring Around the Rosy
- Row, Row, Row Your Boat
- Pop Goes the Weasel
- Here We Go Looby-Loo

Activity 2

Directions: Say, "I know 'Jack and Jill.' I'll bet you do, too. Let's say it together." Then, have the child recite nursery rhymes with you using slow, easy speech. Some suggested nursery rhymes are:

- Jack and Jill
- Baa, Baa, Black Sheep
- Little Boy Blue
- Hickory, Dickory, Dock
- Mary, Mary, Quite Contrary
- Little Jack Horner
- Humpty Dumpty
- Little Miss Muffet
- Old King Cole
- Little Bo Peep

Activity 3

Directions: Say, "I like to do finger plays. Let's do 'Eensy Weensy Spider' together." Then, do finger plays using slow, easy speech and slow movements. Some suggested finger plays are:

- Eensy Weensy Spider
- Way Up in an Apple Tree
- Five Little Firemen Standing in a Row
- Five Little Monkeys Jumping on a Bed
- I Have Two Eyes to See With
- Here is the Church
- There Was a Little Turtle
- Six Little Ducks That I Once Knew
- I'm a Little Teapot

Step 2: Establishing Easy Speech

> Goal: The child will produce words, phrases, and sentences using easy speech in structured modeling tasks.

In this step, the child will practice using easy speech in very structured game activities. Work will progress from words to phrases to short sentences, thus controlling the length of the linguistic component. Work will also progress from imitative to stereotypical and/or carrier sentences to questions and answers to short one-to-two sentence responses. Again, the length of the linguistic component is controlled.

Model slow, easy speech while doing each task (about 90-110 words per minute initially) and use slightly exaggerated inflection patterns. Avoid competitive activities or make sure the activities are set up so the child always wins. Model a positive attitude by saying things like, "It's okay to make mistakes," or "I had fun even though I didn't win." Include an occasional normal disfluency such as a whole word repetition (1-2 times) or a phrase repetition or revision so the child realizes that some disfluency is acceptable.

Two variations of directions are possible in this step depending on the child's age, severity of the problem, or level of awareness. For most young children (ages 2-5) with mild to moderate disfluencies and little awareness of the problem, a totally indirect modeling approach is recommended.

For older children with moderate to severe disfluencies and some awareness, you might consider a direct modeling approach. Explain to the child that there are two ways to talk — a hard way and an easy way. Then, tell the child that you want her to learn to talk the easy way. At this time, you might want to introduce the character, EZ, the animal who only talks using easy speech.

It's not necessary to complete every activity within each objective of this step. Progress through the four objectives in order, but move on to the next objective as soon as you feel confident that the child can successfully complete the objective. In doing so, you may often only use one or two activities at the imitation and stereotyped/carrier response levels (Objectives 1 and 2).

You should, however, use imitation or stereotyped/carrier responses whenever introducing a higher level response to prepare the child for success. For example, when introducing new vocabulary, return to imitation. This allows the child to become familiar with the words before having to say them. Similarly, to prepare the child for Objective 4, use descriptive sentences that focus on attributes (color, shape, size) and functions.

Suggestions for Support Providers

Invite the child's parents/caregivers or teachers to observe and/or participate in an activity or demonstrate how to play the activities. If possible, have them practice so you know they understand how to use easy speech.

Send home copies of the activities in the Materials Book as indicated in each activity. Since a given activity may be used to elicit several response types (e.g., imitative or carrier sentences), it is imperative that you provide explicit directions for the response type to be used at home.

Step 2, *continued*

Encourage parent(s), caregivers, and teachers to have a 5-10 minute quiet time with the child each day to play the games. Share Home Letter #2 and/or Daycare/Preschool Letter #2, pages 102 and 103, so all support people understand the rationale for what will happen during this step.

> **Objective 1:** The child will imitate words, phrases, and sentences using easy speech in structured activities.

Procedure

Model words, phrases, and sentences for the child while participating in structured activities. Then have the child imitate. Initially model a slightly slower rate (about 90-110 words per minute) and a slightly exaggerated inflection pattern (ball ↗, fish ↘, baby ↗↘). Later, model a more normal inflection pattern at a rate which seems to be optimal for eliciting fluency from the child. This rate may be 90-110 words per minute or slightly faster.

Begin by having the child imitate words, then phrases, and then carrier sentences like "I have a (blank), I see a (blank), This is a (blank)," or "Here is a (blank)." Finally, move on to descriptive sentences. Usually you will only need to present 5-10 words before introducing phrases. Then you will often only need 5-10 phrases before moving on to carrier sentences and then descriptive sentences. You may be able to move through all four responses in one activity and go on to an Objective 2 activity.

Indirect modeling: Model the response in easy speech and encourage the child to "say it like I do" or "say what I say."

Direct modeling: Tell the child, "Let's use our easy talking while we play this game. You say what I say using nice, easy speech." Or you might introduce EZ and use the following directions. "This is EZ. There are two ways of talking — a hard, pushing way and an easy way. EZ uses the easy way when he (she) talks. Listen to him (her) talk. Now, let's talk the way EZ does while we play this game."

What if the child is fluent, but doesn't model your rate or inflection? Continue the activity without comment. Simply repeat what the child said using easy speech so she hears the target behavior, but don't demand exact modeling.

What if the child stutters instead of modeling easy speech? Remind the child to "say it like I do (or EZ does)." If the child still stutters, repeat the word or phrase in easy speech and move on to the next response. If the child continues to have trouble, try saying the responses in unison or try using a hand gesture to indicate the inflection pattern. If the child consistently stutters on certain words or words beginning with certain sounds, eliminate them. Re-introduce them once the child has gained some success in modeling.

Activity 1

Materials: purse or shaving kit, comb, toothbrush, toothpaste, hairbrush, etc.

Home Activity: Purse or Shaving Kit, Materials Book, page 8 or 9

Step 2, *continued*

Directions: Take turns pulling items out of the purse or shaving kit. Name each item using easy speech and have the child imitate you. Progress from words (*Key. You say that.*) to phrases (*Big comb. You say that.*) to sentences (*This is a pencil. You say that.*) and finally to descriptive sentences (*I write with a pencil. You say that.*) Drop the prompt "You say that" as soon as the child catches on to the imitative routine.

Activity 2

Materials: ball, car, or truck (Option: pictures of single items)

Home Activity: none

Directions: Roll the ball, car, or truck back and forth while saying words (*fish*) in easy speech. Progress to having the child imitate phrases (*red book*), carrier sentences (*I see a cat*), and descriptive sentences (*Bees make honey*). (Option: Show the child a picture or put a picture in the car or truck as you roll it to the child. Name the item in the picture using easy speech. Encourage the child to roll the car or truck back and say the name of the picture just like you did.)

Activity 3

Materials: box, bag, or can; miscellaneous toy items

Home Activity: none

Directions: Place the toy items and container in front of the child. Choose an item and name it using easy speech. Have the child name the item just like you did and then put it in the container. Next, have the child choose an item. Name the item for the child and encourage her to imitate you. Progress to using phrases (*big ball*), carrier sentences (*Here is a bed*) and then descriptive sentences (*We sit on a chair*).

Activity 4

Materials: grocery bag or basket and toy food

Home Activity: Basket and Food, Materials Book, pages 10-11

Directions: Put the items in the container. Explain to the child that you have some things to show him. Take the items out one at a time and name them using easy speech. Have the child imitate you. Progress from words (*apple*) to phrases (*red apple*) to carrier sentences (*I have an apple*) to descriptive sentences (*We slice an apple*). Let the child take each item and place it on the table or floor.

Activity 5

Materials: pictures from any activity in Objective 2 (Materials Book, pages 23-84)

Home Activity: none

Step 2, *continued*

Directions: Before beginning any game activity from Objective 2, show the child the pictures to be used. Have her imitate you as you name them at the word, phrase, carrier sentence, or descriptive sentence level. If the vocabulary is new, start at the word level and work up to sentences. This way, the child will be familiar with the words before beginning the activity.

Activity 6

Materials: any Unemotional Situation Picture Story or Unemotional Sequence Picture Story, Materials Book, pages 12-22

Home Activity: any Unemotional Situation Picture Story or Unemotional Sequence Picture Story, Materials Book, pages 12-22

Directions: Read the story one sentence at a time using easy speech. Have the child imitate each sentence after you.

Objective 2: The child will produce stereotyped or carrier sentences using easy speech.

Procedure

Have the child participate in structured activities using easy speech to produce carrier and stereotyped sentences. Carrier sentences have parentheses in them to indicate the words used in the parentheses will change (e.g., "I have a (dog), I see a (cat), This is a (cow)," or "Here is a (sheep)"). Stereotyped sentences are said over and over and are not varied (e.g., "Pick a piece," or "It goes here"). Rate should be 90 - 110 words per minute or slightly faster.

Initially, model the sentences and have the child imitate them. Once the child catches on to the pattern, drop the imitation. Alternate turns with the child using the carrier/stereotyped sentences. If the vocabulary items are unfamiliar, have the child imitate them before beginning the task. This will reduce stress on word retrieval during the task.

When playing games, it's important to arrange the pictures so the child wins. Losing is a disrupter and will not be introduced until Step 3. Keep comments about winning like "I'm going to win; I only need one more," to a minimum. When the child wins, say, "You won and I lost. Oh well, I had fun anyway. It's fun to play even if you don't win. Maybe I'll win next time." These comments will provide the child with a good model when he eventually loses, and they also teach good sportsmanship.

Periodically, while naming objects or playing a game, make a mistake and correct yourself (*I found a dog—oh, I mean a cat*). This helps the child realize it is acceptable to make mistakes.

Indirect modeling: Model the response in easy speech. Encourage the child to "say it like I do," or "say what I say."

Direct modeling: Tell the child, "Let's use our easy talking while we play. Say what I say using easy speech." If you are using EZ, say, "Remember how talking can be hard and pushing or easy? Let's use EZ's way of talking, the easy way."

Step 2, *continued*

What if the child won't say the target sentence? If the child simply changes the target (e.g., the child says, "I have a (dog)" instead of "I found a (dog)"), follow the child's lead and model her sentences. If the child won't say structured sentences, simply tell the child, "This is how we play this game." If the child refuses, try modeling a few responses to see if she will join in. If not, try a different activity or have the support person join in to see if this extra model will encourage participation. Remember, even if the child does not respond, she is still hearing an easy speech model which may eventually be internalized.

What if the child misarticulates a word or has dialect differences in pronunciation or form? Accept the child's production but continue to present the model.

What if the child cannot think of the name of an object or picture? Offer a choice such as, "Is it a dog or a cat?"

What if the child engages in irrelevant conversation? The child needs to experience fluency as much as possible. Since fluency is more apt to be present in structured modeling tasks than in conversation, it is important to keep the child on task as much as possible during the early stages of therapy. Tell the child, "Let's play the game now. We can talk later."

What if the child doesn't want to imitate you at the onset of the activities? If the child is fluent during productions, imitation is not necessary.

Activity 1

Materials: any simple puzzle

Home Activity: none

Directions: Put the puzzle pieces between you and the child. Explain that the two of you will be putting a puzzle together. Before beginning, have the child imitate the names of any objects pictured on the puzzle pieces if unfamiliar with them. Say, "This is a (circle). You say that."

Start putting the puzzle together. If the puzzle has pieces which have an object on each piece, include the name of the picture in a carrier sentence. Say, "I pick a piece. It's a (shoe). You say that." Wait for child to say, "It's a (shoe)." Then say, "It goes right here. You say that." Wait for the child's response. "Your turn."

Drop the prompting as soon as possible. If the puzzle does not have an object on each piece, say, "I pick a piece. You say that." Wait. "It goes right here." Wait. "Your turn." If the child does not use the carrier/stereotyped sentences, prompt by saying, "Say, 'I pick a piece.' "

Activity 2

Materials: toy food, basket or cart, paper bags

Home Activity: Basket and Food, Materials Book, pages 10-11

Step 2, *continued*

Directions: Place the toy food between you and the child. Tell the child that the two of you will be buying groceries. Before beginning, have the child imitate the name of each item by saying, "This is a (box of cereal). You say that."

Then pick up one of the items and say the name of the item in a sentence (e.g., "I want a (box of cereal)". Then put the item in the basket or cart and say, "I put it in the basket (cart). Your turn." Alternate turns. Later, you and the child can remove food items from the basket (cart) and place them in paper bags while saying, "I bought a (box of cereal). I put it in the bag."

Activity 3

Materials: purse or shaving kit; objects like keys, toothbrush, and comb

Home Activity: Purse or Shaving Kit, Materials Book, page 8 or 9

Directions: Take everything out of the purse or shaving kit and put it in front of the child. Tell the child that the two of you are going to put things into the purse or shaving kit. Begin by having the child imitate the names of the items.

Pick up one of the items and say, "I found this. This is a (comb)." As you put it in the purse or shaving kit, say, "I put the (comb) in the (purse). Your turn." Alternate turns as you play with the purse or shaving kit.

Activity 4

Materials: toy dishes, a cupboard (or some shoe boxes)

Home Activity: Cupboard and Dishes, Materials Book, pages 23-24

Directions: Put the toy dishes between you and the child. Explain that the two of you will be putting dishes away. Before beginning, have the child imitate the name of each item by saying, "This is a (bowl). You say that."

Start putting the dishes away. Pick up one dish and use its name in a carrier sentence. Say, "I pick a piece. You say that." Wait. Say, "This is a (bowl). You say that." Wait.

As you put the dish in the cupboard say, "I put it right here. You say that." Wait. Then say, "Your turn." If the child doesn't use the carrier/stereotyped sentences during his turn, prompt by saying, "Say . . ."

Activity 5

Materials: toy house, toy furniture

Home Activity: House and Furniture, Materials Book, pages 25-26

Directions: Place the toy house in front of the child. Tell the child that the two of you will be putting furniture into a house. Show the furniture to the child. If the items are unfamiliar, have the child

Step 2, continued

imitate you as you say the name of each item in a sentence. For example, say, "This is a (chair)."

Then, take turns with the child choosing pieces of furniture. Say, "I pick a (chair)." As you put the chair in the house say, "I put it right here. Your turn." Drop the prompts as soon as the child catches on.

Activity 6

Materials: toy dishes, silverware, napkins

Home Activity: Dishes and Silverware, Materials Book, page 27

Directions: Place the toy dishes, silverware, and napkins between you and the child. Explain that it is time to set the table. Before beginning, have the child imitate the names of the items. Say, "This is a (napkin). You say that."

Pick up one of the items and use it in a sentence. Say, "I have a (napkin)." Then put it on the table while saying, "I put it right here. Your turn." Alternate turns using the carrier/stereotyped sentences as you set the table.

Activity 7

Materials: two dolls, doll clothes

Home Activity: Doll and Doll Clothes, Materials Book, pages 28-29

Directions: Place the dolls and doll clothes between you and the child. Tell the child that it is time to dress the dolls. Before beginning, have the child imitate the names of the clothes.

Pick up one of the dolls and one of the clothing items and say, "I have a (shirt). I'll put it on the doll." After you have put the shirt on the doll, say, "Your turn." Alternate turns using the carrier/stereotyped sentences as you dress the dolls.

Activity 8

Materials: tools, toolbox or tool bench

Home Activity: Tools and Toolbox, Materials Book, page 30

Directions: Put the tools and toolbox or tool bench between you and the child. Tell the child that the two of you are going to talk about the tools. Begin by having the child imitate the names of the tools.

Pick up a tool and say, "I picked up a tool. This is a (hammer)." Then say, "We (pound) with a (hammer). Let's put it here. Your turn." Alternate turns using the carrier/stereotyped sentences as you play with the tools.

Activity 9

Materials: toy zoo, zoo animals

Easy Does It For Fluency-Preschool/Primary   Copyright © 1998 LinguiSystems, Inc.

Step 2, continued

Home Activity: Zoo and Zoo Animals 1, Materials Book, pages 31-32

Directions: Place the zoo items between you and the child. Tell the child that the two of you are going to put animals in the zoo. Begin by having the child imitate the names of the animals.

Pick up one of the animals and say, "I found an animal. It is an (elephant)." Then place it in the zoo and say, "The (elephant) goes right here. Your turn." Alternate turns as you play with the zoo.

Activity 10

Materials: toy farm, animals, related objects like tractor and wagon

Home Activity: Farm and Farm Animals 1, Materials Book, pages 33-34

Directions: Place the farm items between you and the child. Tell the child that the two of you are going to put the animals (and related items) on the farm. Begin by having the child imitate the names of the animals and objects.

Pick up one of the objects and say, "I pick a piece. This is a (horse)." As you put it on the farm say, "The (horse) goes here. Your turn." Alternate turns as you play with the farm.

Activity 11

Materials: play cars and trucks, play garage

Home Activity: Garage 1 and Vehicles 1, Materials Book, pages 35-36

Directions: Put the toy garage and the cars and trucks between you and the child. Tell the child that the two of you are going to put the vehicles into the garage.

Pick up one of the vehicles and say, "This is a (truck)." While putting it in the garage say, "I put the (truck) in the garage. Your turn." Alternate turns as you play with the vehicles.

Activity 12

Materials: games and activities such as Colorforms®, Memory®, or Go Fish®

Home Activity: none

Directions: Put the game pieces between you and the child. Be sure to arrange them so that the child wins. Explain the game to the child. Before beginning, have the child imitate the names of the pictures in short sentences.

Play the game using a sequence of carrier/stereotyped sentences such as, "I pick up a card. I found a (number 2). I pick another card. They match/don't match. Your turn." Alternate turns using this sequence throughout the game.

Easy Does It For Fluency-Preschool/Primary   Copyright © 1998 LinguiSystems, Inc.

Step 2, *continued*

Activity 13

Materials: clothes, suitcase

Home Activity: Suitcase, Materials Book, page 37

Directions: Put the clothes and the suitcase between you and the child. Explain that the two of you are going to pack the suitcase. Begin by having the child imitate the names of the clothing items.

Pick up one of the clothing items and say, "I have a (shirt)." While putting it in the suitcase say, "I'll put the (shirt) in the suitcase. Your turn." Alternate turns as you pack the suitcase.

Activity 14

Materials: school box, related objects like pencils and crayons

Home Activity: School Box 1 and School Box 2, Materials Book, pages 38-39

Directions: Put the school box and related objects between you and the child. Tell the child that the two of you are going to get the school box ready for school. Begin by having the child imitate the names of the items.

Pick up one of the associated objects and say, "Here is a (pencil)." While putting it in the school box say, "I put the (pencil) away. Your turn." Alternate turns as you pack the box.

Activity 15

Materials: toy refrigerator, toy stove, play food, pans

Home Activity: Refrigerator and Stove, Food and Pans, Materials Book, pages 40-41

Directions: Put the play food, pans, refrigerator, and stove between you and the child. Explain that the two of you must decide where to put the food and pans. Begin by having the child imitate the names of the items.

Pick up one of the items and say, "I have a (cake pan)." Put the cake pan in the stove and say, "I put it in the stove. Your turn." Alternate turns as you put the food and pans away.

Activity 16

Materials: Mr. and Mrs. Potato Head® and related pieces

Home Activity: Face 1 and Face 2, Materials Book, pages 42-43

Directions: Put Mr. and Mrs. Potato Head® and related pieces between you and the child. Explain that the two of you are going to put the potato heads together. Begin by having the child imitate the names of the items.

Easy Does It For Fluency-Preschool/Primary

Pick up one of the heads and then one of the pieces. Say, "I have a (nose)." While putting it on the head say, "I put the (nose) right here. Your turn." Alternate turns as you complete the heads.

Activity 17

Materials: pan, water, doll, hygiene items (shampoo, towel, washcloth, brush, soap, toothbrush, etc.)

Home Activity: none

Directions: Put the pan of water, the doll, and the hygiene items between you and the child. Tell the child that the two of you are going to clean the doll. Begin by having the child imitate the names of the items.

Pick up the doll and one of the hygiene items and say, "I have a (washcloth)." While washing the doll say, "I'm (washing) the doll's (hair). Your turn." Alternate turns as you clean the doll.

Activity 18

Materials: water, dishes, dishpan, dishcloth, towel

Home Activity: none

Directions: Put the dishpan full of water and the other items between you and the child. Explain that the two of you are going to wash the dishes.

Pick up one of the dishes and say, "I have a (plate). I'm washing the (plate). Your turn." Alternate turns as you wash the dishes.

You may want to expand the activity by drying the dishes. Say "I'm drying the (plate)." When it is dry say, "I'll put the (plate) right here." Alternate turns.

Activity 19

Materials: beads, two strings

Home Activity: none

Directions: Put the beads between you and the child. Explain that the two of you are going to string the beads.

Pick up a string and a bead and say, "I have a bead." Then, while putting it on the string say, "I'm stringing the bead. Your turn." Alternate turns as you string the beads.

Activity 20

Materials: shape sorter, shape pieces

Step 2, *continued*

Home Activity: none

Directions: Put the shape pieces and the shape sorter between you and the child. Explain that the two of you are going to put the shape pieces into the shape sorter. Begin by having the child imitate the names of the shapes.

Pick up one of the shapes and say, "I have a (square)." While putting it in the appropriate hole say, "I put the (square) right here. Your turn." Alternate turns.

Activity 21

Materials: toy vehicles; blue, white, and gray construction paper

Home Activity: Water/Road Scene and Vehicles 2, Materials Book, pages 44-45

Directions: Cut out water using the blue paper, clouds for the sky using the white paper, and a road using the gray paper. Then put the water, clouds, road, and toy vehicles between you and the child. Explain that the two of you are going to decide where each vehicle belongs.

Pick up a vehicle and say, "I have a (boat)." As you put each vehicle in the water or sky, or on the road say, "I put the (boat) on the (water). Your turn." Alternate turns as you place the vehicles.

Activity 22

Materials: playground equipment, play people

Home Activity: Playground and Objects for Playground, Materials Book, pages 46-47

Directions: Place the playground equipment and people between you and the child. Tell the child that the two of you are going to play with the people and the playground equipment. Begin by having the child imitate the names of the equipment and the people.

Pick up one of the pieces of equipment and say, "I have a (swing). I put it here. Your turn." Alternate turns. After all of the playground equipment is in place, take turns putting the children on it. Say, "I have a (boy). I put (him) on the (swing). Your turn." Alternate turns.

Activity 23

Materials: gardening tools

Home Activity: none

Directions: Place the gardening tools between you and the child. Tell the child that the two of you are going to talk about gardening. Begin by having the child imitate the names of the tools.

Pick up one of the tools and say, "I have a (watering can)." Then say, "I (water plants) with a (watering can). Your turn." Alternate turns.

Easy Does It For Fluency-Preschool/Primary

Step 2, *continued*

Activity 24

Materials: sporting equipment

Home Activity: none

Directions: Place the sporting equipment between you and the child. Explain that the two of you are going to talk about the purpose of each piece of sporting equipment. Begin by having the child imitate the names and functions of the sporting equipment.

Pick up one of the pieces of equipment and say, "I have a (bat)." Then say, "I can (hit a ball) with a (bat). Your turn." Alternate turns as you name and describe the items.

Activity 25

Materials: clothing for different genders and ages

Home Activity: People and Clothing, Materials Book, pages 48-49

Directions: Place the clothing between you and the child. Tell the child that the two of you are going to decide who wears each piece of clothing. Talk about how some of the clothing is for a woman, some for a man, some for a girl, some for a boy, and some for a baby. Begin by having the child imitate the names of the items.

Pick up one of the clothing items and say, "I have a (dress)." Then say, "It belongs to the (girl). Your turn to pick some clothes." Alternate turns naming clothes and telling whose they are.

Activity 26

Materials: play community workers, their vehicles, a bag

Home Activity: none

Directions: Place the play community workers in a bag. Put the vehicles between you and the child. Tell the child that the two of you are going to find the vehicle that belongs to each of the community workers. Begin by having the child imitate the names of the items.

Retrieve one of the community workers from the bag and say, "This is a (mail carrier)." While putting the mail carrier in the mail truck say, "I put (her) in the (mail truck). You pick a person." Alternate turns naming each worker and telling which vehicle he/she drives.

Activity 27

Materials: cleaning items (broom, mop, dustpan, dustcloth, vacuum, sponge, etc.)

Home Activity: none

Easy Does It For Fluency-Preschool/Primary

Step 2, *continued*

Directions: Place the cleaning items between you and the child. Tell the child that the two of you are going to talk about the purpose of each cleaning item. Begin by having the child imitate their names. Pick up one of the cleaning items and say, "I have a (dustcloth)." As you begin to use the item say, "I (dust) with a (dustcloth). Your turn." Alternate turns naming items and how they are used.

Activity 28

Materials: toy moving van and furniture

Home Activity: Moving Van and Furniture, Materials Book, pages 50 and 26

Directions: Place the toy moving van and furniture between you and the child. Explain that the two of you are going to help somebody move. Begin by having the child imitate their names.

Pick up one of the pieces of furniture and say, "I have a (chair)." As you put it in the moving van say, "I'll put the (chair) in the truck. Your turn." Alternate turns as you load the items.

Activity 29

Materials: assorted costume jewelry, jewelry box

Home Activity: Jewelry, Materials Book, page 51

Directions: Put the jewelry and the jewelry box between the two of you. Tell the child that the two of you need to organize somebody's jewelry. Begin by having the child imitate the names of the items.

Pick up one of the pieces of jewelry and say, "I have a (ring)." While putting it in the jewelry box say, "I put the (ring) right here. You pick a piece." Alternate turns as you sort the jewelry.

Activity 30

Materials: any set of Association Pictures, Materials Book, pages 52-56

Home Activity: any set of Association Pictures, Materials Book, pages 52-56

Directions: Cut apart the Association Pictures. Divide the Association Pictures into two groups (one pile of people, another pile for associated objects). Lay out all of the object pictures in front of the child and keep the pile of people pictures. Explain that the two of you are going to match the people to the things they use. Begin by having the child imitate the names of all of the pictures.

Place one of the people pictures in front of the child and say, "This is a (baker)." Look for the appropriate object on the table. Say, "The (baker) needs a (cake). Your turn." Alternate turns matching the pictures.

Activity 31

Materials: any Location Picture and the corresponding Object Pictures, Materials Book, pages 57-72

Step 2, continued

Home Activity: any Location Picture and the corresponding Object Pictures, Materials Book, pages 57-72

Directions: Cut apart the Object Pictures. Place a Location Picture in front of the child and put the corresponding Object Pictures beside it. Tell the child that the two of you are going to put people and things on a picture. Begin by imitating their names.

Choose an Object Picture and say, "I pick the (taxi)." Put it on the Location Picture. Then say, "I put the (taxi) right here. Your turn." Alternate turns until all of the Object Pictures are on the Location Picture.

Activity 32

Materials: any two sets of Matching Pictures, Materials Book, pages 73-78

Home Activity: any two sets of Matching Pictures, Materials Book, pages 73-78

Directions: Make two copies of each page. Place one Matching Picture page in front of the child and a different Matching Picture page in front of you. Cut apart the pictures of the other copies. Mix up the pictures you cut apart and place them in a pile between the two of you. Make sure one of your pictures is on the bottom of the pile so the child will win.

Tell the child that the two of you are going to play a matching game. Before beginning, have the child imitate the names of the pictures.

Pick up a picture and say, "I pick a picture. I found a (duck). I need it (you need it)." If the picture matches one of the pictures on your sheet, place it on your sheet. If it matches one of the pictures on the child's sheet, give her the picture to place on her sheet. Alternate turns until the child wins. Talk about how much fun you had even if you didn't win.

Activity 33

Materials: any set of Memory Pictures, Materials Book, pages 79-84

Home Activity: any set of Memory Pictures, Materials Book, pages 79-84

Directions: Make two copies of the pictures and cut them apart. Put 5 - 10 pairs of pictures (depending on the age and ability of the child) facedown between you and the child. Tell the child that the two of you are going to play a memory game.

Pick up a card. Say, "I pick a card. I found a (pear)." Then pick up another card and say, "I pick another card. I found an (apple)." Say, "They don't match," or "They match." The person who makes a match gets to keep the pair. If no match is made, the pictures should be placed back on the table facedown. Alternate turns. Be sure that the child wins the game. Talk about how much fun you had even if you didn't win.

Step 2, continued

Objective 3: The child will ask and answer questions using easy speech.

Procedure

Model questions and answers for the child during structured activities. To ease into these tasks, questions have been added to the previous activities to establish easy speech in carrier or stereotyped sentences. If new items are used that are unfamiliar, be sure to have the child imitate their names before beginning. The rate should be 90-110 words per minute or slightly faster. Initially expect the child to answer your questions after the type of answer has been modeled. After the routine is established, expect the child to ask questions.

Be sure to ask only one question at a time, waiting for an answer before asking the next question. Also, be sure to alternate turns to elicit both answers and questions from the child. If the child forgets to ask the question, use an "Ask me . . ." prompt.

As a reminder, it's important to arrange the pictures so the child wins. When the child wins, make comments such as "Oh, you won. I lost. I had fun even if I didn't win," or "Maybe I'll win next time." Help the child realize that it is okay to make mistakes by making one or two during activities. Be sure to correct them, however, so as not to confuse the child.

Indirect modeling: Model the response in easy speech. Encourage the child to "say it like I do," or "say what I say."

Direct modeling: Tell the child, "Let's use our easy talking while we play. Say what I say in easy speech." If you are using EZ, say, "Remember how talking can be hard and pushing or easy? Let's use EZ's way of talking, the easy way."

What if the child cannot reverse roles for questioning? Try using a visual cue for distinguishing occupations like a picture of a teacher (Materials Book, page 165) and tell the child to pretend to be the teacher. Or have puppets or other characters (e.g., a dog or a cat) play the game and have the child ask the questions for one of the characters.

What if the child misarticulates a word or has dialect differences in pronunciation or form? Accept the child's production but continue to present the correct model.

What if the child cannot think of the name of an object or picture? Offer a choice such as, "Is it a dog or a cat?"

What if the child engages in irrelevant conversation? The child needs to experience fluency as much as possible. Since fluency is more apt to be present in structured modeling tasks than in conversation, it is important to keep the child on task as much as possible during the early stages of therapy. Tell the child, "Let's play the game now. We can talk later."

Step 2, *continued*

Activity 1

Materials: a puzzle with an object on each piece

Home Activity: none

Directions: Put the puzzle pieces between you and the child. Explain that the two of you will be putting a puzzle together.

To work on answering questions, ask "What is this?" as you show the child a piece of the puzzle. Wait for an answer. If the child answers with a single word, say, "Yes. This is a (car). You say that." Then ask, "Where does it go?" Wait for an answer. Again, if the child answers with a single word, say, "It goes here. You say that."

To work on asking questions, alternate turns. Say, "Now you pick a piece and ask me, 'What is this?'" After the child responds, tell the child, "Now, ask me 'Where will you put it?'" Most children will understand the routine quickly so you'll be able to drop the "Now ask me . . ." prompt. If the child has trouble with asking questions, say, "Now, you be the teacher and ask me, 'What is this?'"

Activity 2

Materials: purse or shaving kit; related objects like comb, toothbrush, or pencil

Home Activity: Purse or Shaving Kit, Materials Book, page 8 or 9

Directions: Take everything out of the purse or shaving kit and put the items in front of the child. Tell the child that the two of you are going to put things into the purse or shaving kit.

Pick up one of the items and ask, "What is this?" Then ask, "Where should I put it?" Alternate turns so that the child answers and asks questions.

Expand the activity by telling the child the function of each item. Say "We (brush) (hair) with a (hairbrush)." Then after asking "What is this?," ask "What do we do with a (brush)?"

Activity 3

Materials: toy food, basket or cart

Home Activity: Basket and Food, Materials Book, pages 10-11

Directions: Place the toy food between you and the child. Tell the child that the two of you will be buying groceries.

Pick up one of the items and say, "I want (eggs)." Put the eggs in the grocery basket or cart and say, "I put it in the basket." Ask the child, "What do you want?" Wait for a response. Then ask, "Where did you put it?" Wait for a response. Alternate turns so that the child answers and asks questions.

Step 2, continued

Activity 4

Materials: toy dishes, a cupboard (or some shoe boxes)

Home Activity: Cupboard and Dishes, Materials Book, pages 23-24

Directions: Put the dishes between you and the child. Explain that the two of you will be putting dishes away.

Pick up one dish. Ask, "What is this?" Wait for a response. Then ask, "Where does it go?" Wait for the child to respond. Alternate turns so that the child answers and asks questions.

Activity 5

Materials: toy house, toy furniture

Home Activity: House and Furniture, Materials Book, pages 25-26

Directions: Place the house in front of the child. Tell the child that the two of you will be putting furniture into a house.

Pick up one piece of furniture and ask, "What is this?" Wait for a response. Then ask, "Where does it go?" Wait for the child to respond. Alternate turns so that the child answers and asks questions.

Activity 6

Materials: play dishes, silverware, napkins

Home Activity: Dishes and Silverware, Materials Book, page 27

Directions: Place the play dishes, silverware, and napkins between you and the child. Explain that it is time to set the table.

Take turns setting the table with the child. Ask questions such as "What do you need?" and "Where will you put it?" Alternate turns so that the child answers and asks questions.

Activity 7

Materials: two dolls, doll clothes

Home Activity: Doll and Doll Clothes, Materials Book, pages 28-29

Directions: Place the dolls and doll clothes between you and the child. Tell the child that it's time to dress the dolls.

Take turns dressing the dolls with the child. Ask questions such as "What do you need?" and "Where will you put it?" Alternate turns so that the child answers and asks questions.

Step 2, *continued*

Activity 8

Materials: tools, toolbox or tool bench

Home Activity: Tools and Toolbox, Materials Book, page 30

Directions: Put the tools and toolbox or tool bench between you and the child. Tell the child that the two of you are going to talk about the tools.

Pick up a tool and ask, "What is this?" Then ask, "What do we do with it?" Alternate turns so that the child answers and asks questions.

Activity 9

Materials: toy zoo, zoo animals

Home Activity: Zoo and Zoo Animals 1, Materials Book, pages 31-32

Directions: Place the zoo items between you and the child. Tell the child that the two of you are going to put the animals in the zoo.

Pick up one of the animals and ask, "What is this?" Wait for a response. Then ask, "Where should I put it?" Alternate turns so that the child answers and asks questions.

Activity 10

Materials: toy farm, animals, related objects like a tractor and wagon

Home Activity: Farm and Farm Animals 1, Materials Book, pages 33-34

Directions: Place the farm items between you and the child. Tell the child that the two of you are going to put the animals (and related items) on the farm.

Pick up one of the animals/objects and ask, "What is this?" Wait for a response. Then ask, "Where should I put it?" Alternate turns so that the child answers and asks questions.

Activity 11

Materials: toy cars, trucks, garage

Home Activity: Garage 1 and Vehicles 1, Materials Book, pages 35-36

Directions: Put the toy garage and the cars and trucks between you and the child. Tell the child that the two of you are going to put the vehicles into the garage.

Pick up one of the vehicles and ask, "What is this?" Wait for a response. Then ask, "Where should I put it?" Alternate turns so that the child answers and asks questions.

Easy Does It For Fluency-Preschool/Primary

Step 2, continued

Activity 12

Materials: games and activities such as Colorforms®, Memory®, or Go Fish®

Home Activity: none

Directions: Put the game pieces or cards between you and the child. Be sure to arrange them so that the child wins. Explain the game or activity to the child.

Integrate the questions into short carrier and stereotyped questions related to the activity. For example, if the two of you are playing Go Fish®, you would say, "I have a (penguin). Do you have a (penguin)?" Initially, model a response for the child. Say "No, I don't have a (penguin). Go Fish." or "Yes, I have a (penguin). Here it is." Place all pairs on the table. Alternate turns as you continue to match the pictures.

Activity 13

Materials: clothes, suitcase

Home Activity: Suitcase, Materials Book, page 37

Directions: Put the clothes and the suitcase between you and the child. Explain that the two of you will be packing the suitcase.

Pick up one of the items and ask, "What is this?" Then ask, "Where should I put it?" Alternate turns so that the child answers and asks questions.

Expand the activity by having the child imitate sentences that relate to where each piece of clothing goes on the body. Say "Shoes go on our feet." Then after asking "What is this?," ask "Where do we wear (shoes)?" Complete the activity by asking, "Where should I put them?"

Activity 14

Materials: school box, related objects like pencils and crayons

Home Activity: School Box 1 and School Box 2, Materials Book, pages 38-39

Directions: Put the school box and related objects between you and the child. Tell the child that the two of you are pretending to get ready for school by getting a school box ready.

Pick up one of the related objects and ask, "What is this? " Then ask, "Where should I put it?" Alternate turns so that the child answers and asks questions.

Expand the activity by telling the child the function of each item. Say "I (write) with a (pencil)." Then after asking "What is this?," ask "What do we do with a (pencil)?" Complete the activity by asking, "Where should I put it?"

Easy Does It For Fluency-Preschool/Primary

Step 2, *continued*

Activity 15

Materials: toy food, play pans, refrigerator, stove

Home Activity: Refrigerator and Stove, Food and Pans, Materials Book, pages 40-41

Directions: Put the food, pans, refrigerator, and stove between you and the child. Explain that the two of you are going to decide where to put the items.

Pick up one of the items and ask, "What is this?" Then ask, "Where should I put it?" Alternate turns so that the child answers and asks questions.

Activity 16

Materials: Mr. and Mrs. Potato Head®, related pieces

Home Activity: Face 1 and Face 2, Materials Book, pages 42-43

Directions: Put the Potato Heads and related pieces between you and the child. Explain that the two of you are going to put the Potato Heads together.

Pick up one of the heads and then one of the pieces. Ask, "What do I have?" Then ask, "Where should I put it?" Alternate turns so that the child answers and asks questions.

Activity 17

Materials: pan, water, doll, hygiene items (shampoo, towel, washcloth, brush, soap, toothbrush, etc.)

Home Activity: none

Directions: Put the pan of water, the doll, and the hygiene items between you and the child. Tell the child that the two of you are going to clean the doll.

Pick up the doll and one of the hygiene items and ask, "What do I have?" Then ask, "What should I do?" Alternate turns so that the child answers and asks questions.

Activity 18

Materials: water, dishes, dishpan, dishcloth, towel

Home Activity: none

Directions: Put the dishpan full of water and the other items between you and the child. Explain that the two of you are going to wash the dishes.

Pick up one of the items and ask, "What do I have?" Then ask, "What should I do with it?" Alternate turns so that the child answers and asks questions.

Easy Does It For Fluency-Preschool/Primary

Step 2, *continued*

Activity 19

Materials: beads, two strings

Home Activity: none

Directions: Put the beads between you and the child. Explain that the two of you are going to string the beads.

Pick up a bead and ask, "What do I have?" Then ask, "What should I do with it?" Alternate turns so that the child answers and asks questions.

Activity 20

Materials: shape sorter, shape pieces

Home Activity: none

Directions: Put the shape pieces and the shape sorter between you and the child. Explain that the two of you are going to put the shape pieces into the shape sorter.

Pick up one of the shapes and ask, "What do I have?" Then ask, "Where should I put it?" Alternate turns so that the child answers and asks questions.

Activity 21

Materials: vehicles; blue, white, and gray construction paper

Home Activity: Water/Road Scene and Vehicles 2, Materials Book, pages 44-45

Directions: Use the pretend water, clouds, and road from Objective 2, Activity 21 (page 21) or cut out pretend water using the blue paper, clouds for the sky using the white paper, and a road using the gray paper. Put the water, clouds, and road between you and the child. Explain that the two of you are going to decide where each vehicle belongs.

Pick up a vehicle and ask, "What is this?" Then ask, "Where should I put it?" Alternate turns so that the child answers and asks questions.

Activity 22

Materials: toy playground equipment, play people

Home Activity: Playground and Objects for Playground, Materials Book, pages 46-47

Directions: Place the playground equipment and people between you and the child. Tell the child that the two of you are going to play with the people and the playground equipment.

Step 2, *continued*

Pick up one of the objects and ask, "What is this?" Then ask, "Where should I put it?" Later, choose one of the people and ask, "Where does he want to play?" Alternate turns so that the child answers and asks questions.

Activity 23

Materials: gardening tools

Home Activity: none

Directions: Place the gardening tools between you and the child. Talk about the function of each. Say, "I (dig holes) with a (trowel)." Have the child imitate you.

Tell the child that the two of you are going to talk about the items again. Pick up one of the tools and ask, "What is this?" Then ask, "What do you do with it?" Alternate turns so that the child answers and asks questions.

Activity 24

Materials: sporting equipment

Home Activity: none

Directions: Place the sporting equipment between you and the child. Explain that the two of you are going to talk about each item.

Pick up one of them and ask, "What is this?" Then ask, "What do we do with it?" Alternate turns so that the child answers and asks questions.

Activity 25

Materials: clothing for different genders and ages, play people (woman, man, girl, boy, baby)

Home Activity: People and Clothing, Materials Book, pages 48-49

Directions: Place the clothing and the play people between you and the child. Tell the child that the two of you are going to decide who wears each piece of clothing. Talk about how some of the clothing is for a woman, some for a man, and some for a boy, girl, or baby.

Pick up one of the clothing items like the shoes and ask, "Who is this for?" or "Whose is this?" Then ask, "Where should we put them?" (on the man).

Expand the activity by inserting the question "Where does he wear them?" (on his feet). Alternate turns so that the child answers and asks questions.

Activity 26

Materials: play community workers, their vehicles, a bag

Step 2, *continued*

Home Activity: none

Directions: Place the play community workers in a bag. Put the toy vehicles between you and the child. Tell the child that the two of you are going to find the vehicle that belongs to each community worker.

Take one of the community workers from the bag and ask, "Who is this?" Show the child the vehicles and ask, "Which vehicle is hers?" or "What does she need?" Alternate turns so that the child answers and asks questions.

Activity 27

Materials: cleaning items (broom, mop, dustpan, dustcloth, vacuum, sponge, etc.)

Home Activity: none

Directions: Place the cleaning items between you and the child. Tell the child that the two of you are going to talk about each of the cleaning items. Talk about the function of each. Say, "I (wash) the (floor) with a (mop)." Have the child imitate you.

Tell the child that you are going to talk about the cleaning items again. Pick up one of the cleaning items and ask, "What is this?" Then ask, "What do you do with it?" Alternate turns so that the child answers and asks questions.

Activity 28

Materials: toy moving van and furniture

Home Activity: Moving Van and Furniture, Materials Book, pages 50 and 26

Directions: Place the toy moving van and furniture between you and the child. Explain that the two of you are going to help somebody move.

Pick up one of the pieces of furniture and ask, "What is this?" Then ask, "Where should I put it?" Alternate turns so that the child answers and asks questions.

Activity 29

Materials: costume jewelry, jewelry box

Home Activity: Jewelry, Materials Book, page 51

Directions: Put the jewelry and the jewelry box between you and the child. Tell the child that the two of you need to organize the jewelry.

Pick up one of the pieces of jewelry and ask, "What do I have?" Put it in the jewelry box and ask, "Where did I put it?" Alternate turns so that the child answers and asks questions.

Step 2, *continued*

Activity 30

Materials: any set of Association Pictures, Materials Book, pages 52-56

Home Activity: any set of Association Pictures, Materials Book, pages 52-56

Directions: Cut apart the Association Pictures. Begin by having the child imitate sentences naming the people and their related items. Say, "This is a (barber). He needs (scissors)." Then, divide the Association Pictures into two groups (one pile of people, another pile for associated objects). Lay out all of the object pictures in front of the child and keep the pile of people pictures. Explain that the two of you are going to match the people pictures to the things they use.

Put out one of the people pictures. Ask, "Who is this?" Then ask, "What does he need?" Alternate turns so that the child answers and asks questions.

Activity 31

Materials: any Location Picture and the corresponding Object Pictures, Materials Book, pages 57-72

Home Activity: any Location Picture and the corresponding Object Pictures, Materials Book, pages 57-72

Directions: Cut apart the Object Pictures. Place a Location Picture in front of the child and put the corresponding Object Pictures beside it. Explain to the child that the two of you are going to put things on a picture.

Ask the child to choose an Object Picture. Ask, "What did you pick?" After the child responds, tell the child to put it on the Location Picture. Then ask, "Where did you put it?" Continue until all of the Object Pictures are on the Location Picture. Alternate turns so that the child answers and asks questions.

For added fun, cover your eyes while the child chooses a picture and places it on the Location Picture. Then open your eyes and find the picture the child has placed on the Location Picture. Say, "You chose a (globe). You put it on the (bookshelf)." Alternate turns so that the child closes her eyes and makes statements.

Activity 32

Materials: any two sets of Matching Pictures, Materials Book, pages 73-78

Home Activity: any two sets of Matching Pictures, Materials Book, pages 73-78

Directions: Make two copies of each page. Place one Matching Picture page in front of the child and a different Matching Picture page in front of you. Cut apart the pictures of the other copies. Mix up the pictures you cut apart and place them in a pile facedown between the two of you. Make sure one of your pictures is on the bottom of the pile so the child will win.

Tell the child that the two of you are going to play a matching game. Say, "I pick a picture. I found a (screwdriver)." Then ask, "Do you need it?" The child should respond, "I need it," or "You need it." Alternate turns until the child has matched all of the pictures on her board.

Activity 33

Materials: any set of Memory Pictures, Materials Book, pages 79-84

Home Activity: any set of Memory Pictures, Materials Book, pages 79-84

Directions: Make two copies of the pictures and cut them apart. Put 5 - 10 pairs of pictures (depending on the age and ability of the child) facedown between you and the child. Tell the child that the two of you are going to play a memory game.

Pick up a card. Say, "I pick a card. I found a (tractor)." Then pick up another card and say, "I pick another card. I found another (tractor)." Ask, "Do they match?" The child should respond, "Yes, they match," or "No, they don't match." The person who makes a match gets to keep the pair. If no match is made, the pictures should be placed back on the table facedown. Alternate turns. Be sure that the child wins the game. Talk about how much fun you had even if you didn't win.

Activity 34

Materials: any Unemotional Situation Story, Materials Book, pages 12-16

Home Activity: any Unemotional Situation Story, Materials Book, pages 12-16

Directions: Place a story between you and the child. Tell the child that the two of you are going to retell the story.

Begin by having the child imitate short sentences about the picture(s). Then ask simple questions that relate directly to the story such as "What is this?" Alternate turns so the child answers and asks questions.

Activity 35

Materials: any Unemotional Sequence Story, Materials Book, pages 17-22

Home Activity: any Unemotional Sequence Story, Materials Book, pages 17-22

Directions: Place a story between you and the child. Tell the child that the two of you are going to retell the story.

Begin by having the child imitate short sentences about each of the pictures. Then ask simple questions that relate to the story such as "What's happening in this picture?" Alternate turns so the child answers and asks questions.

Step 2, *continued*

Objective 4: The child will say sentences using easy speech.

Procedure

Once the child is successful producing stereotyped and carrier sentences and can answer and ask questions in structured tasks, work on formulating short sentences, a more difficult task. When creating formulative sentences, be sure to include descriptions (e.g., color, size, shape) and functions.

Initially introduce formulation in tasks which also involve use of stereotyped and carrier sentences. (Tasks written in this format are labeled A.) If the child remains fluent, use a question-and-answer format. (Tasks written in this format are labeled B.) Later in the program, vary formats as doing both would be too repetitive. Finally, combine the formats. If the child doesn't add a formulative sentence, say, "Tell me something about the ___."

Continue to allow the child to win any game activity. Also continue to model positive attitudes as you lose the games. Remember to make an occasional mistake and then correct it so the child isn't confused.

Indirect modeling: Model the response in easy speech. Encourage the child to "say it like I do," or "say what I say."

Direct modeling: Tell the child, "Let's use our easy talking while we play. Say what I say in easy speech." If you are using EZ, say, "Remember how talking can be hard and pushing or easy? Let's use EZ's way of talking, the easy way."

What if the child stutters when trying to say sentences? Discontinue the activity at an appropriate place and re-establish fluency by having the child say a nursery rhyme, sing a song, or do a finger play with you. Then, return to imitative activities as found in Objective 1 or stereotyped responses as found in Objective 2. In later sessions, add some formulative statements without requiring the child to say them. After the child has observed your formulation during two or three tasks, have her attempt to create her own sentences.

What if the child misarticulates a word or has dialect differences in pronunciation or form? Accept the child's production but continue to present the correct model.

What if the child cannot think of the name of an object or picture? Offer a choice such as, "Is it a dog or a cat?"

What if the child engages in irrelevant conversation? The child needs to experience fluency as much as possible. Since fluency is more apt to be present in structured modeling tasks than in conversation, it's important to keep the child on task as much as possible during the early stages of therapy. Tell the child, "Let's play the game now. We can talk later."

What if the child does not want to imitate you at the onset of the activities? If the child is fluent during productions, imitation is not necessary.

Step 2, continued

Activity 1

Materials: puzzle

Home Activity: none

Directions: Put the puzzle pieces between you and the child. Explain that the two of you will be putting a puzzle together.

A. If the puzzle pieces have an object on each piece, include the name of the picture in a carrier sentence. Say, "This is a (car)." Then, say a sentence about the car such as "The (car) is (fast)." Finally, say, "It goes right here. Your turn."

If the puzzle doesn't have an object on each piece, say, "I have a piece." Then describe the piece in a short sentence such as "It's (green and blue)." Finally, say, "It goes right here. Your turn." Alternate turns including a formulative sentence. Cue the child if needed.

B. Repeat the activity. This time, incorporate questions and answers as well as short formulative sentences. If the puzzle pieces have an object on each piece, ask, "What is this?" Wait for an answer. Have the child tell you something about the picture. Finally, ask, "Where does it go?" Wait for an answer. Alternate turns.

Activity 2

Materials: purse or shaving kit; related objects like toothbrush, comb, or keys

Home Activity: Purse or Shaving Kit, Materials Book, page 8 or 9

Directions: Take everything out of the purse or shaving kit and put the items in front of the child. Tell the child that the two of you are going to put things into the purse or shaving kit.

A. Pick up one of the items and say, "This is a (comb)." Then say something about the comb such as "The (comb) is (white)." As you put it in the purse or shaving kit, say, "I put it in the (purse)." Alternate turns.

B. Repeat the activity. Ask, "What is this?" Then say, "Tell me about it." Finally, ask, "Where should I put it?" Alternate turns.

Activity 3

Materials: toy food, basket or cart, paper bags

Home Activity: Basket and Food, Materials Book, pages 10-11

Directions: Place the toy food between you and the child. Tell the child that the two of you will be buying groceries.

Easy Does It For Fluency-Preschool/Primary

A. Pick up one of the items and say the name of the item in a sentence. Say, "I want (soup)." Then, say a sentence. Say, "I like (soup)." Then put the item in a basket or cart and say, "I put it in the (basket). Your turn." Alternate turns.

Later, you and the child can remove food items from the basket and place them in paper bags while saying, "I bought (soup). (Soup tastes good.) I put it in the bag. Your turn." Alternate turns.

B. Repeat the activity incorporating questions and answers as well as formulative sentences. Pick up one of the items and say, "I want (soup)." Make up a short sentence about soup. Put it in the grocery basket and say, "I put it in the (basket)." Ask the child, "What do you want?" and wait for a response. Then say, "Tell me something about (soup)." Finally, ask, "Where did you put it?" Wait for a response. Alternate turns.

Activity 4

Materials: toy dishes, a cupboard (or some shoe boxes)

Home Activity: Cupboard and Dishes, Materials Book, pages 23-24

Directions: Put the toy dishes between you and the child. Explain that the two of you will be putting dishes away.

A. Pick up a dish. Use the object name in a carrier sentence. Say, "This is a (cup)." Say a short sentence about the cup such as "The (cup) is (blue)." As you put the cup in the cupboard say, "I put it right here. Your turn." Alternate turns. Cue the child if needed by saying, "Tell me something about it."

B. Repeat the activity. Incorporate questions and answers as well as short formulative sentences. After picking up a dish ask, "What is this?" Wait for a response. Then say, "Tell me something about it." Then ask, "Where does it go?" Wait for the child to respond. Alternate turns.

Activity 5

Materials: toy house, toy furniture

Home Activity: House and Furniture, Materials Book, pages 25-26

Directions: Place the house and the toy furniture in front of the child. Tell the child that the two of you will be putting furniture into the house.

A. Use the name of the object in a carrier sentence. Say, "This is a (chair)." Then make up a short sentence about the chair such as "The (chair) has (arms)." As you put the item in the house say, "I put it right here. Your turn." Alternate turns. Cue to formulate if needed.

B. Repeat the activity. Incorporate questions and answers as well as formulation. Show the child the objects that go with the house. Ask, "What is this?" Wait for a response. Say, "Tell me something about it." Then ask, "Where does it go?" Wait for the child to respond. Alternate turns.

Step 2, *continued*

Activity 6

Materials: toy dishes, silverware, napkins

Home Activity: Dishes and Silverware, Materials Book, page 27

Directions: Place the toy dishes, silverware, and napkins between you and the child. Explain that it is time to set the table.

A. Pick up one of the items and use it in a sentence. Say, "I have a (fork). A (fork) is (sharp)." Put it on the table while saying, "I put it right here. Your turn." Alternate turns.

B. Repeat the activity. Incorporate questions and answers as well as formulation. Pick up an item and ask, "What do you need?" Then ask the child to say something about it. Finally, ask, "Where will you put it?" Alternate turns.

Activity 7

Materials: two dolls, doll clothes

Home Activity: Doll and Doll Clothes, Materials Book, pages 28-29

Directions: Place the dolls and doll clothes between you and the child. Tell the child that it's time to dress the dolls.

A. Pick up one of the clothing items and use it in a sentence. Say, "I have a (sock)." Then say something about the sock such as "The (sock) is (red)." Finally, say, "I'll put it on the doll." Give the child a doll as you alternate turns.

B. Repeat the activity incorporating questions and answers as well as short formulative sentences. Alternate dressing the dolls and asking questions such as "What do you need?" and "Where will you put it?" Say sentences about each of the clothing items. Alternate turns.

Activity 8

Materials: tools, toolbox or tool bench

Home Activity: Tools and Toolbox, Materials Book, page 30

Directions: Put the tools and toolbox or tool bench between you and the child. Tell the child that the two of you are going to talk about tools.

A. Pick up a tool and say, "This is a (hammer)." Say a descriptive sentence about the hammer such as "The (hammer) is (big)," or "The (hammer) has a (handle)." Then talk about the function. "We (pound) with a (hammer)." Alternate turns.

Step 2, *continued*

B. Repeat the activity incorporating questions and answers as well as short formulative sentences. Pick up a tool and ask, "What is this?" Say, "Tell me something about it." Then ask, "What do we do with it?" Alternate turns.

Activity 9

Materials: toy zoo, zoo animals

Home Activity: Zoo and Zoo Animals 1, Materials Book, pages 31-32

Directions: Place the zoo items between you and the child. Tell the child that the two of you are going to put the animals in the zoo.

A. Pick up one of the animals/objects and say, "This is a (zebra)." Then, say a sentence about the animal/object such as "The (zebra) has (stripes)." Place it in the zoo and say, "The (zebra) goes right here." Alternate turns.

B. Repeat the activity. Incorporate questions and answers and short formulative sentences. Pick up one of the animals/objects and ask, "What is this?" Wait for a response. Then say, "Tell me about it." Finally, ask, "Where should I put it?" Alternate turns.

Activity 10

Materials: toy farm, animals, related objects like a tractor and wagon

Home Activity: Farm and Farm Animals 1, Materials Book, pages 33-34

Directions: Place the farm items between you and the child. Tell the child that the two of you are going to put the animals on the farm.

A. Pick up one of the objects and say, "This is a (horse)." Then say something about the horse such as "The (horse) has (four legs)." As you put it on the farm say, "The (horse) belongs here." Alternate turns.

B. Repeat the activity. Incorporate questions and answers as well as formulative sentences. Pick up one of the animals/objects and ask, "What is this?" Wait for a response. Then say, "Tell me something about it." Finally, ask, "Where should I put it?" Alternate turns.

Activity 11

Materials: cars, trucks, play garage

Home Activity: Garage 1 and Vehicles 1, Materials Book, pages 35-36

Directions: Put the play garage, cars, and trucks between you and the child. Tell the child that the two of you are going to put the vehicles into the garage.

A. Pick up one of the vehicles and say, "This is a (car)." Say something about the car while putting it in the garage such as "I put the (car) in the garage." Alternate turns.

Easy Does It For Fluency-Preschool/Primary

B. Then, pick up one of the vehicles and ask, "What is this?" Wait for a response. Then say something about the item. Finally, ask, "Where should I put it?" Alternate turns.

Activity 12

Materials: games and activities such as Colorforms®, Memory®, or Go Fish®

Home Activity: none

Directions: Put the game pieces between you and the child. Be sure to arrange them so that the child wins. Explain the game or activity to the child.

A. Use the short carrier or stereotyped sentences related to the activity you used earlier. This time incorporate a short formulative sentence as well. For example, if you are playing Memory®, use a sequence of carrier/stereotyped sentences such as "I pick up a card. I found a (cat). The (cat) is (gray). I pick another card. I found a (dog). The (dog) is (brown). They match/don't match." Alternate turns.

B. Repeat the activity. This time, incorporate the previously used questions and answers and also formulative sentences. For example, if you are playing Go Fish®, you could ask, "Do you have a (penguin)?" Wait for a response. Then say something about the penguin such as "The (penguin) is in the (water)." If a match is made, put the pair in a pile beside you. Alternate turns.

Activity 13

Materials: clothes, suitcase

Home Activity: Suitcase, Materials Book, page 37

Directions: Put the clothes and the suitcase between you and the child. Explain that the two of you will be packing the suitcase.

A. Pick up one of the clothing items and say, "I have a (shoe)." Say something about the item while putting it in the suitcase such as "I'll put it in the suitcase." Alternate turns.

B. Then, pick up one of the items and ask, "What is this?" Wait for a response. Then say, "Tell me about it." Finally, ask, "Where should I put it?" Alternate turns.

Activity 14

Materials: school box, related objects like pencils and crayons

Home Activity: School Box 1 and School Box 2, Materials Book, pages 38-39

Directions: Put the school box and related items between you and the child. Tell the child that the two of you are pretending to get ready for school.

A. Pick up one of the related items and say, "This is a (pen)." Then say something about the pen such as "I (write) with a (pen)." While putting the object in the school box, say, "I put it away." Alternate turns.

Step 2, *continued*

B. Repeat the activity. Pick up one of the related items and ask, "What is this?" Wait. Then say, "Tell me about it." Finally, ask, "Where should I put it?" Alternate turns.

Activity 15

Materials: toy food, refrigerator, stove

Home Activity: Refrigerator and Stove, Food and Pans, Materials Book, pages 40-41

Directions: Put the food, the refrigerator, and the stove between you and the child. Explain that the two of you are going to decide where to put the food items.

A. Pick up one of the food items and say, "This is (lettuce)." Say something about it. While putting the food item in the stove or the refrigerator say, "I put it in the (refrigerator)." Alternate turns.

B. Repeat the activity. Pick up one of the food items and ask, "What is this?" Say, "Tell me about it." Wait for a response. Then ask, "Where should I put it?" Alternate turns.

Activity 16

Materials: Mr. and Mrs. Potato Head®, related pieces

Home Activity: Face 1 and Face 2, Materials Book, pages 42-43

Directions: Put Mr. and Mrs. Potato Head® and related pieces between you and the child. Explain that the two of you are going to put the Potato Heads together.

A. Pick up one of the heads and then one of the pieces. Say, "I have a (nose)." Say something about it. Then, while putting the nose on the head say, "I put it right here." Alternate turns.

B. Repeat the activity. Pick up one of the heads and then one of the pieces. Ask, "What do I have?" Wait. Then say, "Tell me something about it." Finally ask, "Where should I put it?" Alternate turns.

Activity 17

Materials: pan, water, doll, hygiene items (shampoo, towel, washcloth, brush, soap, toothbrush, etc.)

Home Activity: none

Directions: Put the pan of water, the doll, and the hygiene items between you and the child. Tell the child that the two of you are going to clean the doll.

A. Pick up the doll and one of the hygiene items and say, "I have a (washcloth)." Say something about it. Then, begin using the item. For example, while washing the doll with the washcloth, say, "I'm washing the doll's (legs)." Alternate turns.

B. Repeat the activity. Pick up the doll and one of the hygiene items and ask, "What do I have?" Then say, "Tell me about it." Finally, ask, "What should I do with it?" Alternate turns.

Step 2, *continued*

Activity 18

Materials: water, dishes, dishpan, dishcloth, towel

Home Activity: none

Directions: Put the dishpan full of water and the other items between you and the child. Explain that the two of you are going to wash the dishes.

A. Pick up one of the items and say, "I have a (bowl)." Then say something about the bowl. Finally, talk about what you're doing such as "I'm washing the (bowl)." Alternate turns.

B. As you are drying the dishes, remember to incorporate questions and answers as well as short formulative sentences. Pick up a dishcloth and ask, "What do I have?" Wait. Then say, "Tell me something about the (bowl)." Finally, ask, "What should I do with it?" Alternate turns.

Activity 19

Materials: beads, two strings

Home Activity: none

Directions: Put the beads between you and the child. Explain that the two of you are going to string the beads.

A. Pick up a bead and say, "I have a bead." Briefly describe the bead. Then, while putting the bead on the string say, "I'm stringing the bead." Alternate turns.

B. Repeat the activity incorporating questions and answers as well as short formulative sentences. Pick up a bead and ask, "What do I have?" Then say, "Tell me something about it." Finally, ask, "What should I do with it?" Alternate turns.

Activity 20

Materials: shape sorter, shape pieces

Home Activity: none

Directions: Put the shape pieces and the shape sorter between you and the child. Explain that the two of you are going to put the shape pieces into the shape sorter.

A. Pick up one of the shapes and say, "I have a (square)." Say a short sentence about it such as "The (square) is (red)." Then, while putting it in the appropriate hole say, "I put it right here." Alternate turns.

B. Repeat the activity. Incorporate questions and answers as well as short formulative sentences. Pick up one of the shapes and ask, "What do I have?" Then say, "Tell me about it." Finally, ask, "Where should I put it?" Alternate turns.

Step 2, *continued*

Activity 21

Materials: vehicles; blue, white, and gray construction paper

Home Activity: Water/Road Scene and Vehicles 2, Materials Book, pages 44-45

Directions: Use the pretend water, clouds, and road from Objective 2, Activity 21 (page 21) or cut out pretend water using the blue paper, clouds for the sky using the white paper, and a road using the gray paper. Put the water, clouds, and road between you and the child. Explain that the two of you are going to decide where each vehicle belongs.

A. Pick up a vehicle and say, "I have a (car)." Say something about it. As you put each vehicle in the water or sky or on the road say, "I put the (car) on the (road)." Alternate turns.

B. Repeat the activity and incorporate questions and answers and short formulative sentences into the activity. Pick up a vehicle and ask, "What is this?" Wait for a response. Then say, "Tell me about it." Finally, ask, "Where should I put it?" Alternate turns.

Activity 22

Materials: toy playground equipment, play people

Home Activity: Playground and Objects for Playground, Materials Book, pages 46-47

Directions: Place the toy playground equipment and people between you and the child. Tell the child that the two of you are going to play with the people on the playground equipment.

A. Pick up one of the people and say, "I have a (boy)." Then say something about the boy. As you place the boy on one of the pieces of playground equipment say, "I put (him) on the (swing)." Alternate turns.

B. Repeat the activity. Incorporate questions and answers as well as short formulative sentences into the activity. Pick up one of the people and ask, "What is this?" Wait for a response. Then say, "Tell me something about (him)." Finally, ask, "Where does (he) want to play?" Alternate turns.

Activity 23

Materials: gardening tools

Home Activity: none

Directions: Place the gardening tools between you and the child. Tell the child that the two of you are going to talk about them.

A. Pick up one of the tools and say, "I have a (rake)." Say something about it. Then talk about what you would do with the object. Say, "I (gather leaves) with a (rake)." Alternate turns.

B. Repeat the activity and incorporate questions and answers and short formulative sentences into the activity. Pick up one of the tools and ask, "What is this?" Wait for a response. Then say, "Tell me something about it." Finally, ask, "What is it for?" Alternate turns.

Step 2, *continued*

Activity 24

Materials: sporting equipment

Home Activity: none

Directions: Place the sporting equipment between you and the child. Explain that the two of you are going to talk about each item.

A. Pick up one of the pieces of equipment and say, "I have a (football). Tell me what it looks like." Then say, "I can (throw) a (football)." Alternate turns.

B. Repeat the activity and incorporate questions and answers and short formulative sentences into the activity. Pick up one of the pieces of equipment and ask, "What is this?" Then say, "Tell me about it." Finally, ask, "What do we do with it?" Alternate turns.

Activity 25

Materials: clothing for different genders and ages

Home Activity: People and Clothing, Materials Book, pages 48-49

Directions: Place the clothing between you and the child. Tell the child that the two of you are going to decide who wears each piece of clothing. Talk about how some of the clothing is for a woman, some for a man, and some for a girl, boy, or baby.

A. Pick up one of the clothing items and say, "I have a (shirt)." Say something about it. Then say, "It belongs to a (man)." Alternate turns.

B. Repeat the activity incorporating questions and answers and formulation. Pick up one of the clothing items and ask, "Who is this for?" Then say, "Tell me about it." Finally, ask, "Where should we put it?" Alternate turns.

Activity 26

Materials: toy community workers, their vehicles, a bag

Home Activity: none

Directions: Place the toy community workers in a bag. Put the vehicles between you and the child. Tell the child that the two of you are going to find the vehicle that belongs to each of the community workers.

A. Take one of the community workers from the bag and say, "Here's a (mail carrier)." Say something about a mail carrier. Then, while putting the mail carrier in the mail truck say, "I put the (mail carrier) in the (mail truck)." Alternate turns.

B. Repeat the activity incorporating questions and answers and formulation. Take one of the community workers from the bag and ask, "Who is this?" Then say, "Tell me about (him)." Finally, show the

Step 2, *continued*

child the vehicles and ask, "Which vehicle is (his)?" Alternate turns.

Activity 27

Materials: cleaning items (broom, mop, dustpan, dustcloth, vacuum, sponge)

Home Activity: none

Directions: Place the cleaning items between you and the child. Tell the child that the two of you are going to talk about each of the cleaning items.

A. Pick up one of the cleaning items and say, "I have a (broom)." Say something about it. Then, as you begin to use the item say, "I (sweep) with a (broom)." Alternate turns.

B. Repeat the activity incorporating questions and answers and formulation. Pick up one of the cleaning items and ask, "What is this?" Say, "Tell me about it." Then ask, "What do we do with it?" Alternate turns.

Activity 28

Materials: play moving van, toy furniture

Home Activity: Moving Van and Furniture, Materials Book, pages 50 and 26

Directions: Place the play moving van and furniture between you and the child. Explain that the two of you are going to help somebody move.

A. Pick up one of the pieces of furniture and say, "I have a (chair)." Say something about the chair. Then, as you put the chair in the moving van say, "I'll put the (chair) in the moving van." Alternate turns.

B. Repeat the activity incorporating questions and answers and formulation. Pick up one of the pieces of furniture and ask, "What is this?" Say, "Tell me about it." Then ask, "Where should I put it?" Alternate turns.

Activity 29

Materials: costume jewelry, jewelry box

Home Activity: Jewelry, Materials Book, page 51

Directions: Tell the child that the two of you need to organize somebody's jewelry. Put the jewelry and the jewelry box between the two of you.

A. Pick up one of the pieces of jewelry and say, "I have a (ring)." Say something about the ring. While putting it in the jewelry box say, "I put the (ring) right here." Alternate turns.

Step 2, *continued*

B. Repeat the activity incorporating questions and answers and formulation. Pick up one of the pieces of jewelry and ask, "What do I have?" Then say, "Tell me about it." Put it in the jewelry box and ask, "Where did I put it?" Alternate turns.

Activity 30

Materials: any set of Association Pictures, Materials Book, pages 52-56

Home Activity: any set of Association Pictures, Materials Book, pages 52-56

Directions: Cut apart the Association Pictures. Divide the Association Pictures into two groups (one pile of people, another pile for associated objects). Lay out all of the object pictures in front of the child and keep the other pile of pictures. Explain that the two of you are going to match the people pictures to the things they use.

A. Put out one of the people pictures. Say, "This is a (doctor)." Describe the person in a short sentence. Then look for an object associated with the person such as "The (doctor) needs a (stethoscope)." Alternate turns.

B. Repeat the activity incorporating questions and answers and formulation. Ask, "Who is this?" Then say, "Tell me something about her." Finally, ask, "What does she need?" Alternate turns.

Activity 31

Materials: any Location Picture and the corresponding Object Pictures, Materials Book, pages 57-72

Home Activity: any Location Picture and the corresponding Object Pictures, Materials Book, pages 57-72

Directions: Cut the Object Pictures apart. Place a Location Picture in front of the child and put the corresponding Object Pictures beside it. Tell the child that the two of you are going to put things on a picture.

A. Choose an Object Picture. Say, "I pick the (cow)." Next, say something about it, such as, "Cows give milk." Then say, "I put it right here," as you put the cow on the Location Picture. Alternate turns. Continue until all of the Object Pictures are on the Location Picture.

B. Repeat the activity incorporating questions and answers and formulation. Tell the child that you are going to close your eyes while the child chooses a picture. Then ask, "What did you pick?" After the child responds, have the child tell you something about the picture. Then have the child put the Object Picture on the Location Picture. Finally ask, "Where did you put it?" Alternate turns until all of the Object Pictures are on the Location Picture.

Activity 32

Materials: any two sets of Matching Pictures, Materials Book, pages 73-78

Home Activity: any two sets of Matching Pictures, Materials Book, pages 73-78

Step 2, *continued*

Directions: Make two copies of each page. Place one Matching Picture in front of the child and one in front of you. Cut apart the pictures of the other copies. Mix up the pictures you cut apart and place them in a pile between the two of you. Make sure one of your pictures is on the bottom of the pile so the child will win. Tell the child that the two of you are going to play a matching game.

A. Say, "I pick a picture. I found a (dog)." Say, "Tell me something about it." Then say, "I need it (you need it)." Alternate turns.

B. Repeat the activity incorporating questions and answers and formulation. Say, "I pick a picture. I found a (dog)." Next say, "Tell me something about it." Then ask, "Do you need it?" Wait for a response ("I need it," or "You need it.") Alternate turns until all the pictures are gone.

Activity 33

Materials: any Memory Pictures, Materials Book, pages 79-84

Home Activity: any Memory Pictures, Materials Book, pages 79-84

Directions: Make two copies of the pictures and cut them apart. Put 5-10 pairs of pictures (depending on the age and ability of the child) facedown between you and the child. Tell the child that the two of you are going to play a memory game.

A. Say, "I pick a card." After picking up the first card, say, "I found a (pig)." Make up a short sentence about it such as "The (pig) is (fat)." Then pick up another card. Say, "I picked another card. I found a (cow). The (cow) is (brown)." Then say, "They match/don't match." Alternate turns. Be sure that the child wins the game. Talk about how much fun you had even if you didn't win.

B. Repeat the activity incorporating questions and answers and formulation. Have the child pick up a card. Ask, "What did you pick?" Say, "Tell me something about it." Then ask the child to pick up another card. Ask, "What did you pick?" Have the child tell you something about it. Finally, ask, "Do they match?" If they do, the child keeps them. If not, they should be placed back on the table facedown. Alternate turns.

Activity 34

Materials: a ball or a car

Home Activity: none

Directions: Roll a ball or a car to the child, make a statement, and then follow it with a parallel question. Have the child answer in complete sentences. For example, say, "I have on blue pants. What do you have on?" The child might answer, "I have on green shorts." The child should answer the question as he rolls the ball or car back to you. Statements might include:

I like to eat . . .   I like to play . . .   I like to go to . . .   I like to drink . . .   I like to visit . . .

My favorite color is . . .   My favorite dinosaur is . . .   My favorite game is . . .   My favorite toy is . . .

Step 3: Desensitizing to Fluency Disrupters

> Goal: The child will produce easy speech in the presence of fluency disrupters.

During this step, continue to model easy speech in structured tasks while gradually introducing fluency disrupters. The child will be expected to continue to model your speech while ignoring the fluency disrupters. By introducing disrupters to the child, it is anticipated that they will be tolerated when they occur in everyday life.

Activities incorporated into earlier sessions will be reintroduced. This time, however, a disrupter will be added. Disrupters include people, noise, movements, interruptions, varying locations, contradictions, time pressures, emotional topics, and competition.

At the onset of sessions, add a disrupter after fluency has been established. Continue using it until signs of impending disfluency are noted or until it is obvious that the disrupter has no effect on the child's fluency. If disfluency occurs, stop using the disrupter until fluency is regained. Then, gradually reintroduce the disrupter.

You need not use a disrupter throughout a session since an intermittent disrupter is often more realistic than a constant one. Intermittent usage will also increase the child's tolerance to the disrupter.

At first, introduce only one disrupter (e.g., noise or other people). Work up to two to four disrupters per session. Do not use the same disrupter in every activity but vary the disrupters within a session. Don't use more than one disrupter in an activity until the child has tolerated each disrupter separately. Use of combined disrupters (more than one per activity) is the last objective introduced.

Disrupters are in an order we have found to be successful for most of the children with whom we have worked. It's important for each disrupter to be introduced in an order appropriate for the child you are working with. Therefore, base the order of presentation on clinical observations and parental report related to the child's needs.

Indirect modeling: Model the response in easy speech. Encourage the child to "say it like I do," or "say what I say."

Direct modeling: Tell the child, "Let's use our easy talking while we play. Say what I say in easy speech." If you are using EZ, say, "Remember how talking can be hard and pushing or easy? Let's use EZ's way of talking, the easy way."

Suggestions for Support Providers

When appropriate, information about use of activities at home or daycare/preschool is provided under the Materials section of each activity. Since a given activity may be used to elicit several response types (e.g., imitative, carrier), it's imperative that you provide explicit directions for the response type to be used when you explain how to use the activity. Remind the parents, caregivers, and/or teachers that it's all right if the child doesn't model a response type exactly.

Share Home Letter #3 and/or Daycare/Preschool Letter #3 (pages 104 and 105) so all support

Step 3, *continued*

providers understand how the disrupters will be used in therapy. These letters also explain that you'll be contacting support providers soon because of the need to practice situations which are felt to be disruptive at home and/or at daycare/preschool.

Objective 1: The child will produce easy speech in the presence of people.

Procedure

To desensitize the child to different people, invite visitors to attend and participate in the sessions. Practice modeling easy speech with visitors prior to inviting them to attend sessions. Initially, have the person (people) you invite observe for a while (one or two activities or possibly a whole session) before participating. As young children may find observers to be disruptive, it may be wise to include them in activities immediately.

Inform visitors prior to the session that you may have to ask them to leave during the session if the child's fluency appears to be breaking down. You may choose to invite a visitor only during the last activity. Then, if fluency is impacted, it will be possible to complete the activity and thank the visitor for coming in a timely manner. After the visitor has participated in another session and the child has maintained fluency, a longer visit may be appropriate.

Talk to parents/caregivers about inviting another child or adult to join in some of the activities at home. Be sure that parents/caregivers understand that this will increase the difficulty of the task and, therefore, they should attempt to eliminate other disrupters by doing the activities in a quiet setting.

What if a visitor doesn't stay on task? Sometimes visitors forget the directions given at the beginning of the session. When this occurs, you might say, "Guess what, (child's name). We forgot to tell (Grandma) that we do our activity first. We wait until we're done to talk."

What if a visitor doesn't use easy speech? If the child becomes disfluent, you might say, "Please use easy speech, (Grandma), just as we do." Otherwise, ignore it for the time being. Later, remind the visitor about the need to use easy speech. It might be helpful to audiotape the session so the visitor can become aware of how her speech differs from the model.

What if the child begins to stutter during the time a visitor is present? Here are options:

a. Finish the activity while continuing to model easy speech. Then, ask the visitor to leave by saying. "That was fun. (Grandma) has to leave now. We'll play a little longer. Maybe (Grandma) can come another day."

b. Begin using unison responses. Say, "(Child's name), let's say these together."

c. Stop the activity and use an Experiencing Activity such as reciting nursery rhymes or singing songs. Say, "Oh my! We forgot to show (Grandma) how we sing. Let's show (her) now." After you are done, resume the activity.

Step 3, continued

Activity 1

Materials: any play-oriented task in Step 2, Objective 2, Activities 1-29; Materials Book, pages 8-11 and pages 23-51

Home Activity: any play-oriented task, Materials Book, pages 8-11 and pages 23-51

Directions: Follow the directions for any of the activities and add a visitor to the session. Adjust the response level to include carrier/stereotyped responses, questions and answers, or short formulative responses as appropriate.

Activity 2

Materials: any picture task in Step 2, Objective 2, Activities 30 or 31; Materials Book, pages 52-72

Home Activity: any picture task, Materials Book, pages 52-72

Directions: Follow the directions for either activity and add a visitor to the session. Adjust the response level to include carrier/stereotyped responses, questions and answers, or short formulative responses as appropriate.

Activity 3

Materials: any picture game in Step 2, Objective 2, Activities 32 or 33; Materials Book, pages 73-84

Home Activity: any picture game, Materials Book, pages 73-84

Directions: Follow the directions for either activity and add a visitor to the session. Adjust the response level to include carrier/stereotyped responses, questions and answers, or short formulative responses as appropriate.

Activity 4

Materials: any story in Step 2, Objective 1, Activity 6; Materials Book, pages 12-22

Home Activity: any story, Materials Book, pages 12-22

Directions: Follow the directions for this activity and add a visitor to the session. Adjust the response level to include questions and answers or short formulative responses as appropriate.

Objective 2: The child will produce easy speech in the presence of nonverbal and verbal noise.

Procedure

To desensitize the child to noise, add competing noise during the activities in this section. Nonverbal

Step 3, *continued*

noise is usually less distracting than verbal noise, so we suggest that nonverbal noise be introduced first. Do not continue the noise throughout the session, but introduce it in only one activity per session.

In subsequent sessions, introduce other noises or vary noises within the activity. While some of the noises you introduce may be regular in beat, make a conscious effort to make some of them irregular. Here are some suggestions to get you started:

- ticking of a minute timer
- typing in the background
- playing audiotapes of environmental sounds
- moving or dropping crayons or paper clips
- tapping a pencil
- tapping a finger on a table

After the child has achieved fluency with nonverbal noise, change to verbal noise. Here are some suggestions to get you started:

- Play unfamiliar vocal songs on a radio or audiotape. If fluency is maintained, play songs familiar to the child.

- Play an audiotape which contains information usually interesting only to adults. If fluency is maintained, introduce an audiotape of interest to the child.

- Turn on a TV show that is of little interest to the child. If fluency is maintained, turn to a program of interest to the child.

Talk to parents/caregivers about introducing noise into home activities. If activities have been completed in quiet settings, have them occasionally leave a TV or radio on. Be sure that parents/caregivers understand that this will increase the difficulty of the task and, therefore, they should attempt to eliminate other disrupters by doing the activities in a quiet setting.

What if the child asks why you are making noise? Say, "Oh, I just wanted to. If it bothers you, I'll stop." Then, reintroduce the noise later in the session. When you do, have the child model responses in imitation before introducing more difficult response types. After you've reintroduced the noise, if the child comments again say, "Oh, I'm sorry. I forgot."

What if the child begins to stutter? Phase out the noise and reestablish fluency. Then, when you reintroduce the noise, have the child model an imitative response before increasing response difficulty.

What if the child doesn't stutter but is upset by the noise and asks you to stop? Tell the child that you are going to continue the noise for a little while longer. Then, continue the noise for a few seconds and stop. Later, reintroduce the noise.

Activity 1

Materials: any play-oriented task in Step 2, Objective 2, Activities 1-29; Materials Book, pages 8-11 and pages 23-51

Home Activity: any play-oriented task, Materials Book, pages 8-11 and pages 23-51

Step 3, *continued*

Directions: Follow the directions for any of the activities and add nonverbal or verbal noise to the session. Adjust the response level to include carrier/stereotyped responses, questions and answers, or short formulative responses as appropriate.

Activity 2

Materials: any picture task in Step 2, Objective 2, Activity 30 or 31; Materials Book, pages 52-72

Home Activity: any picture task, Materials Book, pages 52-72

Directions: Follow the directions for either activity and add verbal or nonverbal noise to the session. Adjust the response level to include carrier/stereotyped responses, questions and answers, or short formulative responses as appropriate.

Activity 3

Materials: any picture game in Step 2, Objective 2, Activity 32 or 33; Materials Book, pages 73-84

Home Activity: any picture game, Materials Book, pages 73-84

Directions: Follow the directions for either activity and add verbal or nonverbal noise to the session. Adjust the response level to include carrier/stereotyped responses, questions and answers, or short formulative responses as appropriate.

Activity 4

Materials: any story in Step 2, Objective 1, Activity 6; Materials Book, pages 12-22

Home Activity: any story, Materials Book, pages 12-22

Directions: Follow the directions for this activity and add verbal or nonverbal noise to the session. Adjust the response level to include questions and answers or short formulative responses as appropriate.

Objective 3: The child will produce easy speech in the presence of movement.

Procedure

To desensitize the child to movement, engage the child in a fine motor task while doing the activities in this section. It is not suggested nor is it recommended that all of the activities be introduced with each of the fine motor tasks listed on the following page. Instead, choose only as many activities and types of fine motor tasks you feel are necessary to feel confident that the child can maintain fluency in the presence of movement.

Many Step 2 activities have movement inherent within the task. The difference in this objective is adding movement to tasks in which movement is NOT inherent. Here are some suggestions to get you started:

- modeling clay or Play Doh®
- coloring
- painting
- putting puzzles together
- pasting

Talk to parents/caregivers about introducing movement into home activities. Tell them to have the child paste, color, model clay, or put puzzles together while imitating a verbal response. Be sure that parents/caregivers understand that this increases the difficulty of the task and, therefore, they should attempt to eliminate other disrupters by doing the activities in a quiet setting.

What if the child begins to stutter while doing the fine motor task? Let the child continue the fine motor task, but stop expecting speech for a while. In a few minutes, reintroduce speech in a unison format (e.g., singing a song, completing a nursery rhyme) or an imitation format.

Activity 1

Materials: any set of Association Pictures, Materials Book, pages 52-56

Home Activity: any set of Association Pictures, Materials Book, pages 52-56

Directions: Cut apart the set of Association Pictures. Show the pictures to the child while he is engaged in a fine motor activity. Have the child imitate a carrier phrase/sentence or descriptive sentence or create a descriptive sentence about the picture pairs.

Activity 2

Materials: any set of Matching Pictures, Materials Book, pages 73-78

Home Activity: any set of Matching Pictures, Materials Book, pages 73-78

Directions: Cut apart the set of Matching Pictures. Show the pictures to the child while he is engaged in a fine motor activity. Have the child imitate carrier phrase/sentence or descriptive sentences or create a descriptive sentence about the pictures.

Activity 3

Materials: any Unemotional Situation or Sequence Story, Materials Book, pages 12-22

Home Activity: any Unemotional Situation or Sequence Story, Materials Book, pages 12-22

Directions: Have the child imitate the storyline while engaging in a fine motor activity.

Step 3, *continued*

> **Objective 4:** The child will produce easy speech in the presence of interruptions.

Procedure

To desensitize the child to disruptions, arrange for interruptions to occur during any of the activities in this section. Do only as many activities as you feel are necessary to desensitize the child to interruptions. Introduce the interruptions while the child is modeling imitative responses before expecting the child to model more difficult response types. Arrange interruptions in the following progression:

- incidental disruptions present because of an open door
- contrived noise interruptions such as dropping pencils or knocking over books
- contrived movement interruptions where you are looking away from the child, moving materials, or getting up and walking around the room
- people interruptions such as having someone knock on the door to talk to you
- verbal interruptions where you interrupt the child once or twice while he is talking to you

Because interruptions are often present within the home, it isn't necessary to send home activities that target this objective.

What if the child begins to stutter? Discontinue the interruptions and reestablish fluency. When interruptions are reintroduced, reduce the response complexity.

Activity 1

Materials: any play-oriented task in Step 2, Objective 2, Activities 1 - 29; Materials Book, pages 8-11 and pages 23-51

Home Activity: none

Directions: Follow the directions for any of the activities and add interruptions to the session. Adjust the response level to include carrier/stereotyped responses, questions and answers, or short formulative responses as appropriate.

Activity 2

Materials: any picture task in Step 2, Objective 2, Activity 30 or 31; Materials Book, pages 52-72

Home Activity: none

Directions: Follow the directions for either activity and add interruptions to the session. Adjust the response level to include carrier/stereotyped responses, questions and answers, or short formulative responses as appropriate.

Step 3, *continued*

Activity 3

Materials: any picture game in Step 2, Objective 2, Activity 32 or 33; Materials Book, pages 73-84

Home Activity: none

Directions: Follow the directions for any of the activities and add interruptions to the session. Adjust the response level to include carrier/stereotyped responses, questions and answers, or short formulative responses as appropriate.

Activity 4

Materials: any Unemotional Situation or Sequence Story in Step 2, Objective 1, Activity 6; Materials Book, pages 12-22

Home Activity: none

Directions: Follow the directions for any of the stories and add interruptions to the session. Adjust the response level to include carrier/stereotyped responses, questions and answers, or short formulative responses as appropriate.

Objective 5: The child will produce easy speech in a variety of locations.

Procedure

To desensitize the child to a change in location while maintaining fluency, arrange for sessions to be held in different locations while completing any of the activities found in this section. Do only as many activities as you feel are necessary to desensitize the child to a change in location. Initially, have the child model imitative responses before modeling more difficult response types. Here are some suggested location changes to get you started:

- just outside of the therapy room
- a different room in the same building
- a different building such as a library or restaurant during a quiet time

Note: Avoid noisy or busy times as they provide combined disrupters.

Suggest that parents/caregivers change where they have been completing activities. Suggest moving to different rooms at home or doing the activity outside of the home. Be sure that parents/caregivers understand that changing locations will increase the difficulty of the task and, therefore, they should attempt to eliminate other disrupters by doing the activities in a quiet setting.

What if the child begins to stutter? Finish the activity as quickly as possible. Then return to the therapy room and establish fluency. Try a change in location at a later time.

Step 3, *continued*

Activity 1

Materials: any play-oriented task in Step 2, Objective 2, Activities 1-29; Materials Book, pages 8-11 and pages 23-51

Home Activity: any play-oriented task, Materials Book, pages 8-11 and pages 23-51

Directions: Follow the directions for any of the activities but change the location of the session. Adjust the response level to include carrier/stereotyped responses, questions and answers, or short formulative responses as appropriate.

Activity 2

Materials: any picture task in Step 2, Objective 2, Activity 30 or 31; Materials Book, pages 52-72

Home Activity: any picture task, Materials Book, pages 52-72

Directions: Follow the directions for either activity but change the location of the session. Adjust the response level to include carrier/stereotyped responses, questions and answers, or short formulative responses as appropriate.

Activity 3

Materials: any picture game in Step 2, Objective 2, Activity 32 or 33; Materials Book, pages 73-84

Home Activity: any picture game, Materials Book, pages 73-84

Directions: Follow the directions for either activity but change the location of the session. Adjust the response level to include carrier/stereotyped responses, questions and answers, or short formulative responses as appropriate.

Activity 4

Materials: any story in Step 2, Objective 1, Activity 6; Materials Book, pages 12-22

Home Activity: any story, Materials Book, pages 12-22

Directions: Follow the directions for this activity but change the location of the session. Adjust the response level to include carrier/stereotyped responses, questions and answers, or short formulative responses as appropriate.

Objective 6: The child will produce easy speech during contradictions.

Procedure

To desensitize the child to the contradictions he'll be facing during everyday speaking activities, introduce

Step 3, *continued*

situations where the child will deal with contradictions while completing any of the activities in this section. Because contradictions tend to be difficult for many children to handle, only introduce contradictions two or three times in an activity.

Introduce two types of contradictions:

1. **Contradicting You**
   If you want the child to contradict (or correct) you, it's necessary for you to make a mistake. For example, you might incorrectly name a picture or incorrectly match two pictures. Acknowledge your mistake if the child corrects you. Say, "Oh, you're right. I made a mistake. I guess I didn't look very well. That's okay." If the child doesn't correct you, wait a turn and say, "Oh look. I made a mistake. I put the pig and the cow together. That's not right. I made a mistake." This type of acknowledgement will help build an attitude that it's okay to make mistakes.

2. **Contradicting the Child**
   To work on contradicting the child, disagree with the child when he names a picture or says he needs one. Wait for the child to defend himself. When he does (or even if he doesn't), acknowledge your mistake like in the example above, so as not to confuse him.

Because contradictions often occur at home, it's not necessary to assign home activities that target this objective.

What if the child begins to stutter? Stop contradictions and reestablish fluency. Reintroduce contradictions at a later date.

Activity 1

Materials: any play-oriented task in Step 2, Objective 2, Activities 1-29; Materials Book, pages 8-11 and pages 23-51

Home Activity: none

Directions: Follow the directions for any of the activities. During the activity, contradict the child. Adjust the response level to include carrier/stereotyped responses, questions and answers, or short formulative responses as appropriate.

Activity 2

Materials: any picture task in Step 2, Objective 2, Activity 30 or 31; Materials Book, pages 52-72

Home Activity: none

Directions: Follow the directions for either activity. During the activity, contradict the child. Adjust the response level to include carrier/stereotyped responses, questions and answers, or short formulative responses as appropriate.

Activity 3

Materials: any picture game in Step 2, Objective 2, Activity 32 or 33; Materials Book, pages 73-84

Step 3, *continued*

Home Activity: none

Directions: Follow the directions for either activity. During the activity, contradict the child. Adjust the response level to include carrier/stereotyped responses, questions and answers, or short formulative responses as appropriate.

Activity 4

Materials: any story in Step 2, Objective 1, Activity 6; Materials Book, pages 12-22

Home Activity: none

Directions: Follow the directions for this activity. During the activity, contradict the child. Adjust the response level to include carrier/stereotyped responses, questions and answers, or short formulative responses as appropriate.

Objective 7: The child will produce easy speech in the presence of time pressures.

Procedure

To desensitize the child to time pressures found in everyday speaking, present various time pressures to the child while completing activities. Introduce only as many activities as you feel are necessary to desensitize the child. Generally, attempt each time pressure with at least two activities:

- increase your rate of speech to a moderate speed
- introduce verbal time pressures

Because time pressures often occur at home, it isn't necessary to send home activities that target this objective.

What if the child begins to stutter? Remove the time pressures and reestablish fluency. Reintroduce time pressures at a later date.

Activity 1

Materials: any play-oriented task in Step 2, Objective 2, Activities 1-29; Materials Book, pages 8-11 and pages 23-51

Home Activity: none

Directions: Follow the directions for any of the activities and add a time pressure to the session. Adjust the response level to include carrier/stereotyped responses, questions and answers, or short formulative responses as appropriate.

Step 3, *continued*

Activity 2

Materials: any picture task in Step 2, Objective 2, Activity 30 or 31; Materials Book, pages 52-72

Home Activity: none

Directions: Follow the directions for either activity and add a time pressure to the session. Adjust the response level to include carrier/stereotyped responses, questions and answers, or short formulative responses as appropriate.

Activity 3

Materials: any picture game in Step 2, Objective 2, Activity 32 or 33; Materials Book, pages 73-84

Home Activity: none

Directions: Follow the directions for either activity and add a time pressure to the session. Adjust the response level to include carrier/stereotyped responses, questions and answers, or short formulative responses as appropriate.

Activity 4

Materials: any story in Step 2, Objective 1, Activity 6; Materials Book, pages 12-22

Home Activity: none

Directions: Follow the directions for this activity and add a time pressure to the session. Adjust the response level to include carrier/stereotyped responses, questions and answers, or short formulative responses as appropriate.

Objective 8: The child will produce easy speech in the presence of emotional topics.

Procedure

During the activities presented in this section, model easy speech as you express your emotions and describe emotional situations for the child in structured tasks. Gradually lead the child into expressing his emotions in short simple statements. Have the child imitate statements prior to formulating.

Ask parents/caregivers to complete activities which involve emotional topics. Be sure that they understand that it may be more difficult for the child to maintain fluency when talking about emotional topics and therefore, they should attempt to eliminate any other disrupters by doing the activities in a quiet setting.

Step 3, *continued*

What if the child stutters? Finish the activity as quickly as possible. Then, change to a unison or imitative task. Reintroduce emotional topics on another day.

Activity 1

Materials: any Emotional Situation Picture, Materials Book, pages 85-89

Home Activity: any Emotional Situation Picture, Materials Book, pages 85-89

Directions: Show the child an Emotional Situation Picture. Tell the child that you want him to help you tell a story associated with the picture.

After reading each sentence, tell the child, "You say that." Then, ask the child questions related to the picture such as "What's happening here?, What caused this?" or "What will happen next?" After you ask a question, wait for a response. Finally, ask the child to tell you something about the picture.

Activity 2

Materials: any set of Emotional Sequence Pictures, Materials Book, pages 90-95

Home Activity: any set of Emotional Sequence Pictures, Materials Book, pages 90-95

Directions: Cut the pictures apart and show them to the child one at a time. Read the first sentence printed on each picture. Next, have the child repeat the sentences. Then read the second sentence and have the child repeat it. Continue until the story has been read.

Ask the child some questions related to each picture such as "What's happening here?" Wait for a response. Show the child the next picture and repeat the question. Finally, ask the child to tell you something about each picture.

Activity 3

Materials: Ask the child to bring photos of his family, his pets, and/or objects like his home or bicycle. Bring similar pictures to share with the child.

Home Activity: none

Directions: Show the child one of your pictures. Describe it in a carrier sentence such as, "I'm going to tell you something about each of my pictures. Here's my first one. 'This is my house.' Now show me one of your pictures. Tell me, 'This is my mom.' " Alternate turns. Vary the carrier sentences you use for each picture.

Activity 4

Materials: Ask the child to bring photos of family events such as a wedding, vacation, or party. Bring similar pictures to share with the child.

Step 3, continued

Home Activity: none

Directions: Show the child one of your pictures. Describe it in a carrier sentence such as "I'm going to tell you something about each of my pictures. Here's my first one. 'This is my birthday. I had a cake.' Now it's your turn. Show me one of your pictures. Tell me something about it." Vary the carrier sentence you use for each picture.

Activity 5

Materials: a ball or a car

Home Activity: none

Directions: Roll a ball or car to the child. Tell the child how you feel about certain things in short sentences. Use different feeling words. Then ask the child to tell about something that makes him feel that way. You might say, "I feel happy when I go to the zoo. When do you feel happy?"

Use the following emotion words in your sentences:

happy	sad
laugh	cry
angry	afraid
like	don't like
like to do	don't like to do

Objective 9: The child will produce easy speech in the presence of competition.

Procedure

During the activities in this section, you'll systematically prepare the child to cope with competition. The child will come close to losing, play in the presence of verbal competition, and finally will lose a game. To tolerate "almost losing," make the game close. To tolerate verbal competition, say things such as "This is a close game," or "Maybe I'll win today."

It's important that the child continue winning until he has succeeded in tolerating almost losing a game as well as playing in the presence of verbal competition. When the child is ready to lose a game, plan two competitive activities for the session and make sure the child wins the second one. Later, while it won't be necessary to have two tasks in one session, the child should always win more than you do.

Talk to parents/caregivers about the need to prepare the child to cope with competition. When doing competitive activities at home, explain that it's necessary to begin by having the child come close to losing and to play in the presence of verbal competition before he loses a game. Remind the parents/caregivers to let the child win more games than he loses.

Step 3, *continued*

What if the child begins to stutter? Eliminate the competition. If the game has been set for you to win and it's not possible to change the setup, increase your positive statements. Say, "Even if I win this game, you'll probably win next time," or "It's fun to play even if you don't win." Then, use Step 1 or 2 tasks to restore fluency.

Activity 1

Materials: any two sets of Matching Pictures, Materials Book, pages 73-78

Home Activity: any two sets of Matching Pictures, Materials Book, pages 73-78

Directions: Make two copies of each page. Place one Matching Picture page in front of the child and a different Matching Picture page in front of you. Cut apart the pictures of the other copies. Mix up the pictures you cut apart and place them in a pile between the two of you.

Say, "I pick a picture. I found a ___." Then ask, "Do you need it?" The child should respond, "I need it," or "You need it." Alternate turns. Initially, have the child come close to losing a game, then play in the presence of verbal competition, and finally, lose a game. When you want the child to lose the game, be sure that one of the child's pictures is on the bottom of the pile.

Activity 2

Materials: any set of Memory Pictures, Materials Book, pages 79-84

Home Activity: any set of Memory Pictures, Materials Book, pages 79-84

Directions: Make two copies of the pictures and cut them apart. Put 5-10 pairs of pictures (depending on the age and ability of the child) facedown between you and the child. Tell the child that the two of you are going to play a memory game.

Pick up a card. Say, "I pick a card. I found a (car)." Then pick up another card and say, "I pick another card. I found a (boat)." Ask, "Do they match?" The child should respond, "They don't match," or "They match." The person who makes a match gets to keep the pair. If no match is made, the pictures should be placed back on the table facedown. Alternate turns. Initially, have the child come close to losing a game, then play in the presence of verbal competition, and finally, lose a game.

Activity 3

Materials: any ready-made game previously played such as Go Fish® or Memory®

Home Activity: none

Directions: Follow the directions for any of the activities. Adjust the response level to include carrier/stereotyped responses, questions and answers, or short formulative responses as appropriate. Initially, have the child come close to losing a game, then play in the presence of verbal competition, and finally, lose a game.

Easy Does It For Fluency-Preschool/Primary

Step 3, *continued*

> **Objective 10:** The child will produce easy speech in the presence of combined disrupters.

Procedure

Now that the child has maintained fluency during the presence of one disrupter, it's time to introduce two or more at the same time. Introduce tasks in an imitative format before progressing to carrier/stereotyped sentences, question and answer, and formulative formats. Here are some suggestions of combined disrupters to get you started:

- combine contradictions and a different location

- combine interruptions and a different location by conducting therapy in a location where interruptions will probably occur (a restaurant at a busy time) or where you can arrange for interruptions to occur

- combine noise and a different location by having therapy in a noisy park or a noisy classroom

- combine competitive activities with a different location

- combine people and contradictions by introducing contradictions in one task on a day when someone has joined the session. Be sure that you have explained what you will be doing to that person so he will know how to respond appropriately.

- combine people and competition by adding verbal competition or allowing the visitor to win a game. Talk to the visitor ahead of time so that he can respond appropriately. Include two competitive tasks within the session and arrange for the child to win the second one.

Because combined disrupters are often present within the home, it's not necessary to send home activities that target this objective.

What if the child stutters? Eliminate one of the disrupters. If fluency is not regained, stop the modeling task and return to an imitated or unison response.

Activity 1

Materials: any play-oriented task in Step 2, Objective 2, Activities 1 - 29; Materials Book, pages 8-11 and pages 23-51

Home Activity: none

Directions: Follow the directions for any of the activities and add a combined disrupter to the session. Adjust the response level to include carrier/stereotyped responses, questions and answers, or short formulative responses as appropriate.

Step 3, *continued*

Activity 2

Materials: any picture task in Step 2, Objective 2, Activity 30 or 31; Materials Book, pages 52-72

Home Activity: none

Directions: Follow the directions for either activity and add a combined disrupter to the session. Adjust the response level to include carrier/stereotyped responses, questions and answers, or short formulative responses as appropriate.

Activity 3

Materials: any picture game in Step 2, Objective 2, Activity 32 or 33; Materials Book, pages 73-84

Home Activity: none

Directions: Follow the directions for either activity and add a combined disrupter to the session. Adjust the response level to include carrier/stereotyped responses, questions and answers, or short formulative responses as appropriate.

Activity 4

Materials: any story in Step 2, Objective 1, Activity 6; Materials Book, pages 12-22

Home Activity: none

Directions: Follow the directions for this activity and add a combined disrupter to the session. Adjust the response level to include carrier/stereotyped responses, questions and answers, or short formulative responses as appropriate.

Step 4: Transferring Fluency

> Goal: The child will use easy speech in real-life situations.

In this step, you'll provide activities in which the child will have an opportunity to transfer the easy talking used in Steps 1-3 into real-life situations. The activities move beyond structured tasks to semi-structured tasks and then to spontaneous speaking tasks. Within the selected tasks, the response types will gradually become more formulative/conversational. The length of responses will also increase, moving from 1-2 sentence levels in structured tasks to several sentences as appropriate in conversational tasks. The activities in this step include situations which are representative of real-life activities for children ages 2-6.

Even though the psychosocial component continues to be addressed, contrived desensitization will no longer be used. At the outset, disrupters should be eliminated or minimized because the complexity of the tasks will be enough for the child to handle. Disrupters will be introduced later within a natural, rather than a contrived framework. For example, you'll invite visitors to participate in carryover tasks or include real-life noises as sessions move to more realistic settings (i.e., the park or playground). As in previous steps, an effort has been made to progress in small increments to insure success. Consequently, transfer tasks should be role-played before actually being attempted whenever possible.

Similarly, the linguistic component has been addressed by organizing the tasks around pragmatic functions of informing, controlling, ritualizing, expressing feelings, and imagining. The child should be encouraged not only to role play herself, but to take on roles of other characters. In this way, the child can try different rates, qualities, pitches, loudness patterns, and styles to learn that she can do many things with her speech mechanism.

As in all preceding steps, the motor component is addressed by modeling easy speech and movements throughout the tasks. Early in transfer, you may find it advantageous to return to a slightly slower rate (e.g., 90-110 wpm) if you have already increased your rate slightly in preceding tasks. As the child achieves success, you can again increase your rate slightly to match the child's comfortable rate. Continue to use a rate that is slightly slower than an adult rate until you're sure that the increased rate isn't disruptive to the child's fluency. Also continue to present a model that uses short simple sentences and frequent pauses as well as a limited number of direct questions.

It isn't necessary to complete all tasks within each objective in this step, but attempt enough tasks to assure mastery of each type of pragmatic function in a variety of situations. Select activities from each objective simultaneously (i.e., a session should include a task from informing, controlling, ritualizing, expressing feelings, and/or imagining). Don't spend an entire session on informing and another session on expressing feelings, etc. Remember, too, that whenever you have the child take on another person's role in role-playing, the child is working on imagining just as she does when engaging in the tasks from the imagining objective (Objective 5).

When introducing transfer tasks, introduce the vocabulary or topic within easier response types such as imitation or carrier sentences. For example, when introducing freeplay with a toy barn, begin by having the child name all of the items in imitation or by alternately naming them using carrier sentences. In fact, one of the easiest ways to begin this step is to use a formulative activity from Step 2 (e.g., a puzzle activity) and simply add some conversation.

Step 4, *continued*

Suggestions for Support Providers

If you have not already obtained input from the people with whom the child is involved, do so at this time.* The information provided by parents, caregivers, and/or teachers will be helpful in planning meaningful transfer tasks.

Continue to invite parents, caregivers, and/or teachers to participate in therapy sessions as appropriate so they learn how to include transfer activities at home or daycare/preschool.

Share Home Letter #4 and/or Daycare/Preschool Letter #4 (pages 106 and 107) so everyone understands the rationale for this step. Provide materials for home activities as indicated. Be sure to give explicit directions on how to set up and participate in the activities in order to enhance chances for successful transfer to real-life situations.

Objective 1: The child will use easy speech while informing.

Procedure

Informing (giving and getting information) activities begin with role-playing real-life situations and end with actual practice in real-life situations. All of the following informative discourse types are common in young children's expressive language experiences and have been included in the activities.

- accounts (narratives where the speaker relates a past experience which the listener did not share)
- recounts (narratives in which both the speaker and listener participated)
- eventcasts (narratives that explain a present or anticipated event)
- fictional stories
- directions for daily routines

In addition, classroom informative activities that involve giving and getting information and asking for clarification have been included.

Puppet plays have also been included as some children seem more willing to engage in verbal interaction within this format than in role-playing. When using puppets, model the whole dialogue first, taking both parts. Then, have the child choose one of the parts and do the dialogue again. If the child is still interested, switch roles and do the dialogue one more time. Finally, ask the child to recreate both parts. Since these dialogues are very routine and the task so repetitive, it is relatively simple to move into more interactive dialogues, continuing to talk for the puppets without a script. Be sure to model easy speech throughout your dialogue.

What if the child cannot recall the steps in accounts, recounts, eventcasts, and directions? Prompt the child by asking leading questions.

---

* *Family information lists found in* The Fluency Companion, *also published by LinguiSystems, 1994, may be used or you can create your own.*

Step 4, *continued*

What if the child cannot recall the entire story? Prompt with leading questions, or alternate turns with each of you saying a line or two and then allowing the other to say a line or two. Gradually decrease the amount of prompting you provide as the child becomes more capable of retelling the story.

What if the child cannot recall the steps or dialogues verbatim? Do not be concerned. While it is anticipated that the tasks will enhance language development, the focus is on eliciting fluency. Follow the child's lead. For example, if the puppet dialogue states that the character ordered a hamburger but the child says cheeseburger, accept the child's version. It's not necessary to correct or require exact replications. Be sure parents, caregivers, and teachers realize this, too.

What if the child becomes disfluent in the transfer tasks? There are a number of options, but the key is to simplify the task to regain fluency. You might return to a more structured format which involves carrier/stereotyped responses instead of formulative responses; you might shorten the number of responses by alternating turns after one or two sentences instead of after several; or you might interrupt the activity and engage in an experiencing activity. You'll need to do this in a subtle way. For example, you might say, "Guess what? We forgot to sing today. Let's do it now. Then we can play again."

When first introducing transfer tasks be sure to alternate between structured establishing tasks and transfer tasks or use establishing procedures to set up the transfer tasks to enhance chances for success (e.g., have the child name objects in carrier phrases before engaging in conversation about them).

What if the child wants to talk about other stories or events? Follow the child's lead. Encourage the child to bring in favorite stories or relate home/school activities and modify them as needed. If the child becomes disfluent, return to structured tasks as soon as possible, or, if you anticipate that this will be difficult, try to structure the task to enhance chances for success before allowing the child to start. For example, if the child wants to tell you about what happened on vacation, say, "I want to hear all about it, but first let me tell you what I did." Then, use easy speech to tell a short recount of your own. This way, the child has time to relax and to hear an easy speech model before starting.

Note: Avoid any food activities unless the parent has signed a food release form (Materials Book, page 96).

Activity 1

Materials: pitcher, fruit drink mix, water, glasses, spoon, signed food release form, Materials Book, page 96

Home Activity: none

Directions: Begin by describing how to make the fruit drink, using easy speech as you identify the items needed and the steps involved. Have the child imitate your statements ("To make our drink, we need a pitcher. You tell me that. We . . .") or answer simple questions ("To make our drink, we need a pitcher. What do we need?").

After all of the items and steps have been described, have the child help make the fruit drink. Be sure to present a model for easy speech throughout the task. When done, ask the child to tell you the steps involved in making the drink. Provide sequencing prompts if needed ("Good. Then what did we do?"). Then, drink the juice and engage in easy conversation.

Step 4, *continued*

To expand this recount to an account, invite a parent/significant other to join the session and have the child retell the steps.

Activity 2

Materials: Shapes, Materials Book, page 97; colored construction paper; blank sheet of white paper; paste or glue

Home Activity: completed shape scene

Directions: Cut out the shapes from construction paper as indicated. Show the child the shapes. Name the shapes and colors and have the child imitate your sentences ("This is a green circle. You say that.") or ask questions ("This is a green circle. What is this?").

Then, show the child how to make a picture using the shapes. Model easy speech throughout. Emphasize sequence and spatial terms ("First, we put the red square here. Then we put the black triangle on top."). When the picture is completed, have the child give you a recount of what you made together.

To expand this recount to an account, invite a parent/significant other to join the session and have the child retell the steps.

Activity 3

Materials: bread, peanut butter, jelly, spoon, knife, signed food release form, Materials Book, page 96

Home Activity: none

Directions: Begin by naming the items needed. Describe the steps to make a peanut butter and jelly sandwich. Use the method described in Activities 1 and 2 to elicit imitative and short answer responses. Then, make the sandwich together, modeling easy speech throughout.

When the sandwich is completed, have the child give you a recount of the steps involved. Then, eat the sandwiches and engage in easy conversation.

To expand this recount to an account, invite a parent/significant other to join the session and have the child retell the steps.

Activity 4

Materials: none

Home Activity: none

Directions: At the end of a session, review all of the activities you and the child have participated in that day using easy speech. Then, have the child retell what the two of you did. To simplify this task, follow the directions for Activity 5.

Step 4, *continued*

To expand this recount to an account, invite a parent/significant other to join the session and have the child retell the steps.

Activity 5

Materials: Daily Activities Chart, Materials Book, page 98

Home Activity: completed chart

Directions: Before the session, complete the chart with a list of activities for that day. Use picture cues whenever possible (e.g., house for a home activity; phone for a phone activity, etc.). Show the child the chart at the beginning of the session and model easy speech as you describe each activity ("Today we're going to play with the house. Next we'll play with the phones. Then we'll . . . Last we will . . .").

Then, ask the child to tell you what you will be doing that day using the chart as a guide. If needed, prompt by saying, "What will we do first?" At the end of the session, review the chart and ask the child to recount the day's activities.

Invite a parent/significant other to join the end of the session and have the child retell the activities again. Send the chart home so the child can tell about the activities to others. Prompt the child as needed and tell the parent/significant other to do so at home, too.

Activity 6

Materials: any set of Routine Sequence Pictures, Materials Book, pages 99-100

Home Activity: any set of Routine Sequence Pictures, Materials Book, pages 99-100

Directions: Show the child the Routine Sequence Pictures and model the steps for the sequence. For example, say, "These pictures show how to do laundry. First we sort the clothes. Next we put in the laundry detergent. Then we put in the clothes." Have the child imitate each statement or answer a question like "What do we do first?" If you have access to a play laundry set or if you wish to make a washer and dryer from cardboard boxes, you can act out doing the laundry while modeling easy speech.

After you're finished, mix up the pictures and have the child help you arrange them in order. Then, ask the child to tell you the steps, using the pictures as a guide. Prompt the child if needed.

For the child who is capable of retelling the sequence without picture cues, encourage the child to do so or to retell the sequence on another day. If the child remains fluent, lead the child into a discussion on the topic ("I'll bet you help with laundry at home").

To expand this recount to an account, have the child use the pictures to retell the steps for a parent/significant other at the end of the session or at home.

Activity 7

Materials: toy picnic basket, food, dishes, tableware, napkins, tablecloth or blanket

Step 4, *continued*

Home Activity: none

Directions: Tell the child, "Today we're going to have a picnic. First, we have to pack the basket. Here's what we need." (Name the items and have the child imitate the words or answer questions about them such as "What is this?" or "What else do we need?") "Next, we have to drive to the park. Then we'll put out the blanket and set the table. Finally, we'll eat the food. Now, before we do this, tell me again what we're going to do."

Prompt the child with sequence words if needed ("What will we do first?") After the child has produced the eventcast, role-play going on a picnic, modeling easy speech throughout.

When you're finished, have the child give you a recount of the picnic. Then, to expand the recount to an account, have the child tell a parent/significant other about your picnic.

Activity 8

Materials: suitcase, clothes, toiletries

Home Activity: Suitcase, Materials Book, page 37

Directions: Tell the child, "Today we're going to pretend we're going to spend the night at ____'s house. First, we have to pack the suitcase. Here's what we'll need." (Name the items and have the child imitate the words or answer questions such as "What is this?" or "What else do we need?".) "Next we'll put the suitcase in the car. Then we'll drive to ____'s house. Now, before we pretend, tell me again what we're going to do."

Prompt the child with sequence words if needed. After the child has produced the eventcast, role-play packing the suitcase and going to ____'s house, modeling easy speech throughout.

When you're finished, have the child give you a recount of the activity. Then, to expand the recount to an account, have the child tell a parent/significant other about packing the suitcase.

Activity 9

Materials: any Unemotional Situation, Sequence, or Rebus story/pictures, Materials Book, pages 12-22 or 101-104

Home Activity: any Unemotional Situation, Sequence, or Rebus story/pictures, Materials Book, pages 12-22 or 101-104

Directions: Review a story by retelling the story in easy speech. Then, ask the child to retell the story using the pictures as a guide. You may also use any other stories from this step (Step 4) for retelling, but don't introduce emotional stories until the child has first succeeded in retelling unemotional stories.

When the child has completed a story retelling, engage the child in conversation about the story actions or characters.

Step 4, *continued*

Activity 10

Materials: any child-selected book, pictures, or posters that illustrate a familiar story

Home Activity: none

Directions: Have the child retell the story using the book, pictures, or poster as a guide. Prompt the child as needed. When done, engage the child in conversation about the story actions or characters.

Activity 11

Materials: any Familiar Story Sequence Pictures ("Goldilocks and the Three Bears," "The Three Little Pigs," "The Three Billy Goats Gruff") and Familiar Story Lines, Materials Book, pages 105-110

Home Activity: any Familiar Story Sequence Pictures and Familiar Story Lines, Materials Book, pages 105-110

Directions: Model the story using easy speech while showing the sequence pictures. Pause after each picture and point out the items. Be sure to include variations in pitch, loudness, and quality as appropriate for the characters. Then, encourage the child to retell the story. Prompt as needed or alternate telling what happens in each part.

Activity 12

Materials: none or props as appropriate for the situation

Home Activity: none

Directions: Act out the following situations, creating appropriate dialogue. Model easy speech throughout.

- child and parent wrapping a present
- child and grandparent preparing to go fishing
- child and sibling making peanut butter and jelly sandwiches
- child and friend making a birthday card
- child telling parent about preschool
- child and dad making supper
- child and mom making a birdhouse
- child and grandparent making cookies

Activity 13

Materials: any Classroom Informing Story picture, Materials Book, pages 111-113

Home Activity: any Classroom Informing Story picture, Materials Book, pages 111-113

Step 4, *continued*

Directions: Show the child the Classroom Informing Story picture. Read the story using easy speech. Ask the child to retell the story. After the child has finished, engage the child in a conversation about the topic.

Activity 14

Materials: puppets (boy/girl, man/dad, librarian, teacher), Materials Book, pages 114-117 and 164-166

Home Activity: Family Puppets 1-4 (as needed), Community Worker Puppets 1-3 (as needed), Puppet Dialogues: Informing, Materials Book, pages 114-118 and 164-167

Directions: Act out the following classroom situations. Model both parts first. Then, have the child play the child's part. Later, reverse roles. Model easy speech throughout.

Giving Information: Parents' Night
  Child: This is my room.
  Dad: Where is your desk?
  Child: In the front.
  Dad: Which one?
  Child: The one with my name.
  Dad: But I see two with your name.
  Child: Mine has a ball on it.
  Dad: Oh, I see it. Can I sit in it?
  Child: Oh, you are too big.

Clarifying Information: Library
  Librarian: Hi. May I help you?
  Child: Yes. I want that book.
  Librarian: Which book? The one on the second shelf?
  Child: No. The one on the top.
  Librarian: Which one? The one about horses?
  Child: No. The one about dinosaurs.
  Librarian: Oh, that's a good one. I'll get it for you. Do you want to check it out?
  Child: Yes, please. I want to show my sister.

Asking for Directions: Snack Time
  Teacher: It's your turn to pass out snacks.
  Child: What do I do?
  Teacher: First, pass out the cups and napkins.
  Child: What next?
  Teacher: Get the cookies from the cupboard. Put one on each napkin.
  Child: What do I do after that?
  Teacher: Get the juice from the cooler. I'll help you pour it.
  Child: Okay. Can I start?
  Teacher: Yes. Thank you.
  Child: You're welcome. I like to help.

Easy Does It For Fluency-Preschool/Primary

Step 4, *continued*

Activity 15

Materials: paper, crayons

Home Activity: none

Directions: Engage the child in free conversation while coloring. Make leading comments or statements to encourage conversation from the child. Model easy speech throughout. Here are some suggestions to get you started:

Draw a park.
   I like to go to the park. I like to swing.
   I like to ride my bike in the summer.
   I like to feed the birds.

Draw a beach.
   I like to swim in the summer.
   I like to build sand castles.
   I put sunscreen on so I don't get burned.

Draw a winter scene.
   I like to make snowpeople.
   Sometimes I go sled riding.
   I'm not very good at ice skating.

Draw a fall scene.
   I like to rake leaves.
   Last year, we jumped in piles of leaves.
   Once I went on a hayrack ride.

Draw an animal.
   I have a pet cat.
   My dog likes to chase squirrels.
   I got a hamster last week.

Draw a picture of a community worker.
   A firefighter came to school last week.
   I wish I could ride in an ambulance.

Objective 2: The child will use easy speech while controlling.

Procedure

Activities in this objective are designed to provide practice using easy speech while engaging in controlling activities (i.e., activities in which the child's speech is used to control others or the situation). The child will be encouraged to ask for help, give warnings, make promises, give directions, negotiate, state intentions, and offer suggestions and reminders. Some activities begin with structured tasks to introduce the idea of controlling, but move into a conversational mode through retelling of stories, role-playing, and/or puppetry. Model easy speech throughout the tasks.

What if the child cannot remember the exact dialogue? Don't become concerned. Follow the child's lead. Be sure parents/significant others understand this.

What if the child becomes disfluent? Simplify the task by returning to a simpler response type (e.g., carrier/stereotyped responses) or shorter response type (e.g., alternate turns after only one to two sentences). If the child becomes very disfluent, end the task as quickly as possible and introduce a simpler task. Attempt the transfer task again at a later time.

Step 4, *continued*

What if the child doesn't seem to understand role-playing? Try to include some props to make the situation more realistic. Be sure to describe the situations first using easy speech and include dialogue statements so the child will have an idea what to say when role-playing.

Activity 1

Materials: any Controlling Story picture, Materials Book, pages 119-126

Home Activity: any Controlling Story picture, Materials Book, pages 119-126

Directions: While showing the child a controlling picture, tell the child the story. Have the child retell the story. When finished, engage in conversation about the topic.

Activity 2

Materials: puppets from Materials Book, pages 114-117; props if necessary

Home Activity: Family Puppets 1-4 (as needed) and Puppet Dialogues: Controlling, Materials Book, pages 114-117 and 127-129

Directions: Do the following puppet plays. Model the entire dialogue first. Then, have the child select one puppet and act out the play together. Add original dialogue to the end of the dialogue.

Going to the Park: Warning
  Mom: Let's go the park.
  Child: Hurrah!
  Mom: Slow down and watch out for cars.
  Child: Okay. I'm looking both ways.
  Mom: Great. No cars coming. We can cross.
  Child: I want to go on the slide.
  Mom: Be careful. It's really high.
  Child: Catch me, Mommy.
  Mom: Okay. I'm ready. Come down.
  Child: Wheee! That was fun.

Playtime: Negotiating
  Girl: I have two cars.
  Boy: I have two trucks.
  Girl: I wish I had a truck. Want to trade?
  Boy: I'll give you my red truck. Can I have your blue car?
  Girl: Okay.
  Boy: Thanks. Let's pretend we need gas.
  Girl: Okay. Where's the gas station?

Visit: Reminder
  Grandma: Are you ready to come to my house?
  Child: I'm all packed.
  Grandma: Great. Did you remember your toothbrush?

Step 4, *continued*

Child: Oh, no. It's in the bathroom. I'll get it.
Grandma: Now we are ready. Where's your teddy?
Child: He's in my suitcase.
Grandma: Then let's get going.
Child: Did you remember to buy some cake for me?
Grandma: I thought we would go to the bake shop on the way home.
Child: Yay! Can I get cookies?
Grandma: Maybe. Let's go.

Playmates: Suggestions
Girl: Hi!
Friend: Hi!
Girl: What do you want to do?
Friend: Let's play outside.
Girl: We can't. It's raining.
Friend: What do you want to do?
Girl: We could do puzzles.
Friend: I don't like puzzles.
Girl: How about coloring? We could color and listen to my music tapes.
Friend: Okay. I like to color.

Helping: Promise
Mom: I have to go downstairs to do the laundry. Will you watch the baby?
Boy: Sure.
Mom: Will you stay right here until I come back?
Boy: I promise. I'll play with him.
Mom: Great. I knew I could count on you.
Boy: I'll make sure he's safe. I promise.

Leaving: Intention
Child: Where are you going?
Dad: I'm going to get my keys.
Child: Why?
Dad: I'm going to McDonald's.
Child: Why?
Dad: Because I'm hungry. Want to come?
Child: Yes. I'm hungry, too.
Dad: Now, where are you going?
Child: To get my hat.

Snack: Asking for Help
Girl: Let's have milk and cookies.
Boy: Okay. Where are the cookies?
Girl: On the counter.
Boy: I can't reach them. Help me, please.
Girl: Stand on this stool.
Boy: Okay. Where are the glasses?
Girl: I got the glasses, but I can't lift the milk. Help me, please.
Boy: Okay. We can lift it together.

Step 4, *continued*

Classroom: Negotiating
  Cy: Mr. Pete, Tom and I both want the dump truck.
  Mr. Pete: Who had it last?
  Cy: I did.
  Mr. Pete: How about letting Tom have it now? You can have the fire truck.
  Cy: But I like the dump truck better.
  Mr. Pete: We have to share. Maybe you and Tom can switch after while.
  Cy: Okay.

Playground: Negotiating
  Kathy: Let's play tag.
  Callie: I don't want to. Let's build in the sand.
  Kathy: That's messy.
  Callie: I'll play tag now, but then will you play in the sand with me?
  Kathy: Okay.

Activity 3

Materials: Shapes, Materials Book, page 97; colored construction paper; scissors; paste or glue

Home Activity: completed shape scene

Directions: Cut out the shapes using the colored construction paper. Invite a visitor to attend the session. Have the child tell the visitor how to make a shape picture. If needed, prompt the child to give directions by saying, "You could tell (name) to get the blue circle."

Activity 4

Materials: pitcher, glasses, spoon, fruit drink mix, water

Home Activity: none

Directions: Invite a visitor to attend the session. Have the child tell the visitor how to make the fruit drink. If needed, prompt the child to give directions by saying, "You could tell (name) to open the fruit juice mix."

Activity 5

Materials: suitcase, clothes, toiletries

Home Activity: Suitcase, Materials Book, page 37

Directions: Invite a visitor to attend the session. Put the objects around the room. Have the child tell the visitor how to pack the suitcase. Prompt the child if needed as noted above.

Step 4, *continued*

Activity 6

Materials: picnic basket, food, dishes

Home Activity: basket and objects, Materials Book, pages 10-11

Directions: Invite a visitor to attend the session. Have the child tell the visitor how to pack the picnic basket. Prompt the child if needed as noted above.

Activity 7

Materials: puppets (lifeguard, boy/girl, firefighter, police officer, mom/dad, teacher) from the Materials Book, pages 114-117 and 164-166

Home Activity: Family and Community Worker Puppets (as needed), Materials Book, pages 114-117 and 164-166

Directions: Create your own dialogues for the following situations. Model easy speech throughout. Be sure to reverse roles so the child can take on other characters' roles.

- lifeguard warning child at beach
- firefighter warning child about fires
- police officer warning child about strangers
- parent warning child about kitchen dangers (hot stove, sharp knives)
- teacher warning child about classroom dangers (running, sharp pencils)
- parent warning child about tools in workshop
- child promising parent to feed pet
- child promising parent to clean room
- parent promising child to go to movies

Activity 8

Materials: none

Home Activity: none

Directions: Take the child on field trips to places where he can practice easy speech while engaging in controlling tasks. For example, go to the library, the park, the mall, the gym, or the cafeteria and role-play or engage in real-life activities. Model easy speech throughout. On the way, sing songs or recite rhymes to relax the child or describe what you will be doing.

Step 4, *continued*

> **Objective 3:** The child will use easy speech while ritualizing.

Procedure

In this objective, activities will focus on practicing easy speech in situations where the child engages in rituals associated with introductions, greetings and departures, invitations, phone usage, classroom rituals, restaurants, public places, and parties. Practice appropriate dialogue within the framework of story retellings, role-playing, and puppetry. Include field trips to real-life situations whenever possible. Model easy speech throughout. Activities should progress from semi-structured formats to free conversation to spontaneous fluency in real-life situations.

What if the child has trouble remembering dialogues? Don't be concerned. Follow the child's lead if the changes are minor. Prompt the child if necessary, but don't be rigid about exact wordings. The focus is on fluency, not on the dialogue.

What if the child becomes disfluent? Find ways to simplify the task or bring the task to an end. Reestablish fluency and reattempt the task.

What if the child can't think of anything to say in role-playing? Try adding props to make it seem more realistic. Switch to puppets. Some children converse more readily when playing a puppet role than when being themselves.

What if the child is fluent on play phones but not on real ones? End the conversation as quickly as possible and try again after more role-playing practice. You might try engaging in a fluency-enhancing task such as singing or reciting rhymes on the phone and then begin conversing again.

Activity 1

Materials: any Classroom Ritualizing Story, Materials Book, pages 130-133

Home Activity: any Classroom Ritualizing Story, Materials Book, pages 130-133

Directions: While showing the picture, read a Classroom Ritualizing Story using easy speech. Have the child answer simple questions about the story and then, have the child retell the story. Then, ask the child to act out the story with you. When you're finished, engage the child in conversation about the topic.

Activity 2

Materials: Classroom Ritualizing Dialogues (next page); Family and Community Worker Puppets (as needed), Materials Book, pages 114-117 and 164-166

Home Activity: Family and Community Worker Puppets (as needed), Classroom Dialogues (as needed), Materials Book, pages 114-117, 134-135, and 164-166

Step 4, *continued*

Directions: Act out any of the Classroom Ritualizing Dialogues using puppets. Present the dialogue with both puppets first. Then, have the child select a puppet and act out the story together. Reverse roles to give the child a chance to take on another role. When you're finished, engage the puppets in conversation about the topic.

Greetings
   Sherry: Hi, Manny. How are you?
   Manny: Hi, Sherry. I'm fine, but I'm all wet. How are you?
   Sherry: I'm all wet, too. I was jumping in the puddles.
   Manny: I didn't jump in puddles, but I forgot my umbrella.
   Sherry: Oh, well. We'll dry off soon.
   Manny: Yeah, let's go play.

Greetings
   Teacher: Good morning, Buddy. How are you today?
   Buddy: I'm fine. How are you?
   Teacher: I'm fine. I'm sure we'll have a good day.
   Buddy: I brought my spaceman for "Show and Share."
   Teacher: Great. Put it by my desk until it's time.
   Buddy: Okay.

Introduction
   Teacher: Hello. I'm Mr. Romano. I'm your new teacher. What's your name?
   Paula: I'm Paula Ramirez.
   Teacher: I'm happy to have you in class, Paula. Here is your chair.
   Paula: Where do I put my coat?
   Teacher: There is a cubby right here for your coat and other things.
   Paula: Thank you.

Introduction
   Craig: Hi, I'm Craig. Are you lost?
   Nick: Hi. I'm Nick. I don't know. I'm new.
   Craig: This is Miss Field's room. Is she your teacher?
   Nick: Yes.
   Craig: Then this is your class. Miss Field will be right back.
   Nick: Okay. Where do I put my coat?
   Craig: Right here. Come sit by me.
   Nick: Okay. Thanks.

Snack Time
   Mimi: Do you want some juice?
   Juan: Yes, please.
   Mimi: Do you want some cookies?
   Juan: What kind are they?
   Mimi: Chocolate chip.
   Juan: Yes, please. I love chocolate chip cookies.

Step 4, continued

Departure
Teacher: It's time to clean up, boys and girls.
Tina: I'm ready.
Teacher: Great. Don't forget to take your papers home.
Tina: Can I take my folder home, too?
Teacher: Yes. Just be sure to bring it back. Have a nice evening.
Tina: Thanks. See you tomorrow.

Departure
Peter: It's time to go.
Jeff: I'll see you tomorrow.
Peter: Don't forget to bring your bear for "Show and Share."
Jeff: I won't. What will you bring?
Peter: I don't know. I have to hurry. My bus is here.
Jeff: Bye.
Peter: Bye. See you tomorrow.

Turn Taking
Teacher: It's time to go outside. We need to line up.
Laura: Who gets to go first?
Teacher: The boys went first yesterday. Today girls go first.
Laura: Who goes first tomorrow?
Teacher: I think we will go by rows tomorrow. The quiet row will go first.
Laura: I hope my row is first.
Teacher: It will be if you are all quiet.

Calendar
Teacher: Cindy, it's your turn to do the calendar. What day is today?
Cindy: Today is Wednesday.
Teacher: That's right. What month is it?
Cindy: This is May.
Teacher: Good. What should we put on the calendar?
Cindy: We need a sun. It's hot today.

Activity 3

Materials: any Community/Home Ritualizing Story, Materials Book, pages 136-139

Home Activity: any Community/Home Ritualizing Story, Materials Book, pages 136-139

Directions: Read any of the situation stories using easy speech. Have the child answer simple questions about the story. Next, have the child retell the story. Then, ask the child to act out the story with you. When you're finished, engage the child in conversation about the topic.

Activity 4

Materials: Community/Home Ritualizing Dialogues; Family and Community Worker Puppets (as needed), Materials Book, pages 114-117, 141-142, and 164-166

Step 4, continued

Home Activity: Family and Community Worker Puppets (as needed), Community/Home Dialogues (as needed), Materials Book, pages 114-117, 141-142, and 164-166

Directions: Act out any of the Community Situation stories using puppets. Present the dialogue with both puppets first. Next, have the child select a puppet and act out the story together. Reverse roles to give the child a chance to take on another role. Then, engage the puppets in conversation about the topic.

Gas Station
    Dad: We need gas.
    Todd: Can I help pump it?
    Dad: Sure. Help me hold the handle.
    Todd: Can I pay?
    Dad: Okay. Tell the clerk, "Pump 3."
    Todd: Will you come with me?
    Dad: Of course. I'll be right beside you.

Gas Station
    Attendant: Can I help you?
    Todd: I want to pay.
    Attendant: Which pump?
    Todd: Pump 3.
    Attendant: That will be $10.
    Todd: Here's my money.
    Attendant: Here's the change. Do you get it?
    Todd: No. Give it to my dad.

Sports Event
    Vendor: Anyone want a hat?
    Kristen: I want a hat.
    Vendor: What color?
    Kristen: I like blue.
    Vendor: That will be $2.
    Kristen: Okay. Here's my money.
    Vendor: Thank you. Here's your change and your hat.
    Kristen: Thanks.

Fast-food Restaurant
    Counter clerk: May I help you?
    Sarah: I want a hamburger.
    Counter clerk: Do you want something to drink?
    Sarah: I want a root beer and my mom wants coffee with cream.
    Counter clerk: The cream is by the napkins.
    Sarah: I want a pie, too.
    Counter clerk: What kind?
    Sarah: Cherry.
    Counter clerk: Is that all?
    Sarah: Yes.
    Counter Clerk: Here's your food. That's $6.
    Sarah: Here's my money. Thank you.

Step 4, continued

Laundromat
- **Mom:** I wonder where the change machine is.
- **Eddie:** I saw it by the door.
- **Mom:** Oh, good. Help me put the clothes in the washer.
- **Eddie:** Can I pour the detergent in?
- **Mom:** Sure, but let me help you hold it.
- **Eddie:** Can I have a drink?
- **Mom:** I'll buy you some juice when I get the change. Just wait a minute.
- **Eddie:** Okay.
- **Mom:** Here's your juice.
- **Eddie:** Can I push in the money?
- **Mom:** Sure. I'll put it in. Now you push.
- **Eddie:** This is fun!

Activity 5

Materials: toy phones, hand puppets or dolls

Home Activity: Phone Dialogues (as needed), Materials Book, page 142

Directions: Using hand puppets or dolls, present the following phone conversations using easy speech. Then, have the child choose a puppet or doll and repeat the dialogue. When you are finished, engage in some free conversation.

Invitation
- **Sally:** Hello.
- **Sue:** Hi Sally. This is Sue.
- **Sally:** Can you come over to play?
- **Sue:** I can't come. My grandma is here.
- **Sally:** What are you doing?
- **Sue:** We're going to the movies. Want to come?
- **Sally:** I'll ask my Mom. (Pause) It's okay, I can go.
- **Sue:** Great!! Come on over.

(To elicit spontaneous conversation, ask "Have you ever gone to a movie?" or comment, "I'll bet you like to go to movies.")

Birthday
- **Grandpa:** Hello.
- **Child:** Hi Grandpa. Happy Birthday!
- **Grandpa:** Thank you, honey.
- **Child:** Did you get my present?
- **Grandpa:** Yes. That was a great picture. I love it. Thank you so much.
- **Child:** Can you come over? Mom and I made a cake.
- **Grandpa:** I'd love to come over. Grammie and I will be right there.
- **Child:** Bye. I love you.
- **Grandpa:** I love you, too.

(To elicit conversation, ask "Have you ever had a birthday party?" or comment, "I'll bet you've been to a party.")

Easy Does It For Fluency-Preschool/Primary

Game

    Aunt Jean: Hello.
    Child: Hi Aunt Jean. Can you come to my ball game?
    Aunt Jean: I'd love to come. What time?
    Child: Five o'clock.
    Aunt Jean: Where is it?
    Child: At Stephens Park. I got a new uniform.
    Aunt Jean: What color is it?
    Child: Pink and grey.
    Aunt Jean: I'll look for you.
    Child: Okay, bye.
    Aunt Jean: Bye.

(To elicit conversation, ask "Have you ever played ball?" or comment, "I liked to play ball when I was little. I'll bet you like to play games, too.")

Activity 6

Materials: toy phones

Home Activity: none

Directions: Create original dialogues using the following lines to begin the conversations with the person listed. Model easy speech throughout. Introduce the activity by saying, "Let's pretend to call (name). I'll be (name) and you be you. When I say, 'Ring-ring,' you say, 'Hello.' "

Parent
    I forgot my lunch.
    When will you be home?
    Can I stay at Grandma's house tonight?
    I don't feel well.
    Can I go to a movie with (name)?

Friend
    Can you come to my birthday party?
    Do you want to go skating?
    Do you want to go to story hour with us?
    Can you come over?
    Can you spend the night?

Grandparent
    Guess what? I got a kitty today.
    Can you baby-sit me tonight?
    Did I leave my teddy at your house?
    Can you come to my school tomorrow?
    I got my hair cut today.

Step 4, *continued*

Activity 7

Materials: toy phones

Home Activity: none

Directions: Invite a visitor to attend the session. Model any of the dialogues from Activity 5 with the child. Then, invite the visitor to take on your role in the dialogue.

Activity 8

Materials: real phones; a parent/significant other at home

Home Activity: none

Directions: Before the session, arrange for a parent/significant other to be at home. Role-play the call first. Then, have the child call and tell the person what he is doing. Model easy speaking throughout.

Activity 9

Materials: real phones

Home Activity: none

Directions: To give the child practice answering the phone, arrange with the parent for the child to be home at a certain time. Call the child and talk about a familiar topic. If the parent doesn't want the child to answer the phone, arrange for the parent to answer and then, have the child come to the phone to talk.

Activity 10

Materials: none

Home Activity: none

Directions: Take the child on field trips to places such as the library, a fast-food restaurant, donut shop, or ice cream store where he can practice ritualizing. Practice what the child will say on the way to the new location. If you go to a location where you will order something, be the first to order using easy speech so the child hears your model.

Step 4, *continued*

> **Objective 4:** The child will use easy speech while expressing feelings.

Procedure

The activities in this objective provide opportunities to practice easy talking while engaging in situations where expressing feelings is necessary. Activities include story retelling, role-playing, puppetry, and free play. Model easy speaking throughout.

What if the child varies from the dialogues? Don't become concerned. Follow the child's lead.

What if the child becomes disfluent? Simplify the task by returning to more structured responses, shorter responses, or less complex responses, or use a fluency-enhancing technique (e.g., singing, reciting rhymes, or doing an imitative task) and then return to the transfer task.

Activity 1

Materials: any Emotional Situation, Sequence, or Rebus Story, Materials Book, pages 85-95 and 143-146

Home Activity: any Emotional Situation, Sequence, or Rebus Story, Materials Book, pages 85-95 and 143-146

Directions: Review the emotional story using easy speech. Then, ask the child to retell the story. Prompt the child if necessary. When you have finished, elicit conversation about the topic.

Activity 2

Materials: any Classroom Feeling Story, Materials Book, pages 147-150

Home Activity: any Classroom Feeling Story, Materials Book, pages 147-150

Directions: Show the child the picture that illustrates the story. Using easy speech, tell the story. Ask the child to retell the story. When you have finished, engage the child in conversation about the topic.

Activity 3

Materials: Family and Community Worker Puppets, Materials Book, pages 114-117 and 164-166

Home Activity: Family and Community Worker Puppets (as needed) and Classroom Feeling Dialogues (as needed), Materials Book, pages 114-117, 164-166, and 151

Directions: Act out either of the dialogues on the next page which involve classroom situations where one character expresses feelings. Role-play both roles while modeling easy speech. Then, have the child take on one role. Reverse roles. When you are finished, engage the child in conversation about the topic.

Easy Does It For Fluency-Preschool/Primary

Step 4, *continued*

Apology
Let's pretend Tara and Holly are playing ball. Tara accidentally hits Holly with the ball.
Holly: Ow! (pretend to cry)
Tara: Oh, Holly. I'm sorry. I didn't mean to hit you.
Holly: I know. It's okay.
Tara: Does it hurt?
Holly: Just a little.
Tara: Maybe you should rub it.
Holly: That feels better. I'm okay now. Let's play some more.
Tara: Okay.

Sick
Teacher: What's wrong, Pedro?
Pedro: I don't feel good.
Teacher: Do you have a stomachache?
Pedro: No, my throat hurts.
Teacher: You feel warm. I'll call your mother. Maybe someone can come to get you.
Pedro: My grandma will come.
Teacher: Why don't you put your head down? You can rest until someone comes.
Pedro: Okay.
Teacher: Pedro, your grandma is here.
Pedro: Can I go home now?
Teacher: Yes. Take your book bag.
Pedro: Bye. I'll be back tomorrow.
Teacher: Bye, Pedro. I hope you feel better.

Activity 4

Materials: any Community/Home Feeling Story, Materials Book, pages 152-155

Home Activity: any Community/Home Feeling Story, Materials Book, pages 152-155

Directions: Show the child the picture associated with the story. Tell the story using easy speech. Then, ask the child to retell the story. When you're finished, engage the child in conversation about the topic.

Activity 5

Materials: Family and Community Worker Puppets (as needed), Materials Book, pages 114-117 and 164-166

Home Activity: Family and Community Worker Puppets (as needed) and Community/Home Feeling Dialogues, Materials Book, pages 114-117, 164-166, and 156

Directions: Act out any of the dialogues on the next page which involve home situations where one character expresses feelings. Role-play both roles modeling easy speech. Then, have the child take on one role. Reverse roles. When you're finished, engage the child in conversation about the topic.

Sick
Mom: What's wrong, Chad?
Chad: My stomach hurts.
Mom: Let me feel you. You don't feel feverish.
Chad: My head hurts, too.
Mom: Maybe I should take your temperature.
Chad: Will it hurt?
Mom: No. (Wait.) Well, you don't have a fever. Maybe you should rest a while.
Chad: Will you read me a story?
Mom: Sure. Crawl in bed and I'll read you a good story.

Sad
Grammie: What's wrong, Mia?
Mia: My gerbil died.
Grammie: Oh, dear. That's too bad.
Mia: What should we do?
Grammie: Well, let's have a funeral.
Mia: How do we do that?
Grammie: Here's a shoe box. Put your gerbil in here.
Mia: Now what?
Grammie: Get the shovel and let's go out back.
Mia: Where should we bury it?
Grammie: Right behind the garage. I'll dig a hole.
Mia: I'll put the box in and cover it up. Bye-bye, Fuzzy. I'll miss you.

Excitement
Josh: I'm so happy.
Carrie: Why?
Josh: Aunt Meg and my cousin, Peggy, are coming today.
Carrie: What will you do?
Josh: We're going to have a picnic.
Carrie: That sounds like fun.
Josh: Yeah, we're going swimming, too.
Carrie: Have fun.
Josh: Thanks.

Fear
Kellie: What's that noise?
Uncle Joe: That's thunder.
Kellie: I don't like it. It scares me.
Uncle Joe: Don't worry. It can't hurt you.
Kellie: But it's so loud.
Uncle Joe: How about if I hold you on my lap and read you a story?
Kellie: Okay.

Step 4, *continued*

Activity 6

Materials: Preference Pictures, Materials Book, pages 157-158; blank sheets of paper; stapler; paste or glue

Home Activity: completed Preference Book

Directions: Cut apart the pictures. Explain to the child that you're going to make a preference book of all her favorite things. Show the child the pairs of pictures and ask which one she likes better. Have the child glue or paste the preferred picture on the blank sheets. When you are finished, staple the pages together.

While making the book, model easy speech while talking (e.g., I like ice cream better than cake because it's cold).

Activity 7

Materials: paper, crayons

Home Activity: completed drawing

Directions: Engage in conversation while drawing together. Encourage the child to express preferences for colors and things to draw. Model easy speech throughout.

Activity 8

Materials: any toy with pieces about which the child can express preferences such as a toy zoo and animals, barn and animals, toolbox and tools, or grocery cart and groceries

Home Activity: none

Directions: Have the child choose a toy to play with. Encourage the child to express preferences as to the pieces she wants, where she wants to put them, what she wants them to do, etc. Model easy speech throughout, making leading statements to keep the conversation going. For example, you might say, "I like elephants. I wish I could ride on an elephant. I want to put my elephant by the water. I'll bet you have a favorite animal."

Activity 9

Materials: paper, crayons

Home Activity: completed drawing

Directions: Engage the child in free conversation while coloring. Introduce emotional topics such as the following. If you are aware of emotional topics related to the child, work them into your conversations. Model easy speech throughout. Make leading comments or statements and wait for the child to respond.

Draw a sad child.
   This boy is sad. He dropped his Popsicle®.
   This girl is sad. She lost her money.

Easy Does It For Fluency-Preschool/Primary

Draw a car smashed into a tree.
   I was in an accident once, but I didn't get hurt.
   I always wear my seatbelt.
   I saw an ambulance yesterday. It was going fast.

Draw an airplane or van.
   I rode on an airplane once.
   We drove our van to the mountains.
   I like to go on vacations. Once we went camping.
   I like to go to amusement parks. I really like roller coasters.
   Sometimes we go to the lake. Then I ride in a boat.

Draw a party.
   I like to open presents.
   We went bowling for my birthday.
   I like to eat chocolate cake and ice cream.

Draw a crib.
   I have a little baby at my house.
   Sometimes babies cry a lot.
   I like to feed babies.
   Babies can get into your toys sometimes.

Activity 10

Materials: family pictures from the child, clinician pictures

Home Activity: none

Directions: Using pictures from Step 3, Objective 8, Activities 3 and 4, take turns describing the people, objects, and events using carrier sentences. Then, lead the child into a discussion of the events. Model a description of your event (*On my birthday, we went to a park.*). Lead the child into a description of the events in her pictures by making leading comments such as, "I'll bet you had a party for your birthday."

Objective 5: The child will use easy speech while imagining.

Procedure

Activities in this session involve having the child practice easy speech in imaginative dialogue in which she takes on another person's role. The child has already worked on this objective in Objective 4 whenever she and the clinician reversed roles in puppet play or role-playing. Additional role-playing activities are included in this objective.

Step 4, continued

Activity 1

Materials: any Story Puppets and Familiar Story Sequence Pictures, Materials Book, pages 159-160 and 105-107

Home Activity: any Story Puppets and Familiar Story Sequence Pictures, Materials Book, pages 159-160 and 105-107; any Familiar Story Dialogues, Materials Book, pages 161-163

Directions: Place one set of Familiar Story Sequence Pictures in front of the child. Set up the puppets for the story or make them into finger puppets. Explain to the child, "Today we're going to act out ("The Three Little Pigs"). I'll show you first and then we can do it together." Give dialogue for the puppets and only as much story line as needed to keep the story going. Then, ask the child to help you.

Have the child choose the part(s) she wants to play. Provide the necessary story line and alternate turns providing the dialogue. Model easy speech throughout. Be sure to include variations in pitch, loudness, and quality as appropriate for the characters.

Goldilocks and the Three Bears
Mama: Let's go for a walk.
Papa: Okay.
Goldilocks: What a pretty house. I think I'll go in.

Goldilocks sees the porridge and says: I'm hungry. This cereal is too hot. This is too cold. This is great.

Goldilocks goes into the living room and says: This chair is too hard. This chair is too soft. This chair is just right. (Rocks) Oh no. I broke it. Now I'm tired.

Goldilocks goes upstairs and says: This bed is too hard. This bed is too soft. This bed is just right. **She falls asleep and the bears come home.**
Papa: Who's been eating my cereal?
Mama: Who's been eating my cereal?
Baby: Someone's been eating my cereal and it's all gone.

They go in the living room.
Papa: Someone's been sitting in my chair.
Mama: Someone's been sitting in my chair.
Baby: Someone's been sitting in my chair and it's broken.

They go upstairs.
Papa: Who's been sleeping in my bed?
Mama: Who's been sleeping in my bed?
Baby: Someone's been sleeping in my bed and there she is!
Goldilocks: "Oh no. I have to go home."

Easy Does It For Fluency-Preschool/Primary

The Three Little Pigs

Pig 1: I'm building a house of straw.
Pig 2: I'm building a house of sticks.
Pig 3: I'm building a house of bricks.

Wolf to Pig 1: I'm hungry. Let me in.
Pig 1: No.
Wolf: Then I'll huff and puff and blow your house down.

Wolf to Pig 2: I'm hungry. Let me in.
Pig 2: No.
Wolf: Then I'll huff and puff and blow your house in.

Wolf to Pig 3: I'm hungry. Let me in.
Pig 3: No.
Wolf: Then I'll huff and puff and blow your house in.
Pig 3: You can't blow my house in.

So, the wolf tries to climb down the chimney.
Pig 3: Let's catch the wolf. Put a big kettle in the fireplace. (Wait.) There, we caught the wolf. Let's ship him to the zoo.

Three Billy Goats Gruff

Baby Goat: (Speak in a little voice.) I'm hungry. I'm going across the bridge. Clip-clop, clip-clop.
Troll: Who's crossing my bridge?
Baby Goat: I am. Little Billy Goat Gruff.
Troll: I'm going to eat you.
Baby Goat: Don't eat me. I'm little. Wait for my brother.
Troll: Okay.

Middle Goat: (Speak in a medium voice.) I'm hungry. I'm going across the bridge. Clip-clop, clip-clop.
Troll: Who's crossing my bridge?
Middle Goat: I am. Middle Billy Goat Gruff.
Troll: I'm going to eat you.
Middle Goat: Don't eat me. I'm little. Wait for my big brother.
Troll: Okay.

Big Goat: (Speak in a big voice.) I'm hungry. I'm going across the bridge. Clip-clop, clip-clop.
Troll: Who's crossing my bridge?
Big Goat: I am. Big Billy Goat Gruff.
Troll: I'm going to eat you.
Big Goat: No, you aren't. (Have goat bump troll so troll disappears.)

Activity 2

Materials: dress-up clothes or community worker hats

Step 4, continued

Home Activity: none

Directions: Show the child the dress-up clothes or hats. Say to the child, "Today we're going to pretend. Let's put on some clothes and pretend to be people who help us." Lead the child into a conversation by making comments such as "I'm a doctor. I help sick people." Continue describing things a doctor has/does. Then say, "I wonder who you are. What do you do?"

Have the child pretend to be people such as the following: mother, father, grandfather, grandmother, police officer, firefighter, store clerk, teacher, waiter/waitress, fast-food counter worker, custodian, doctor, nurse, receptionist, bus driver, librarian, ticket seller, or gas station attendant. Model easy speech throughout.

Activity 3

Materials: any Community Worker Puppets and Community Worker Monologues, Materials Book, pages 164-167

Home Activity: any Community Worker Puppets and Community Worker Monologues, Materials Book, pages 164-167

Directions: Select a community worker puppet and present a monologue using easy speech in which the puppet describes his job. Have the child take the puppet and retell the monologue using easy speech.

Then, model a monologue for another puppet. If the child is fluent on the first monologue, skip having the child retell the second monologue. Allow the child to select a new puppet and create an original monologue. If you feel this will be too difficult, continue to have the child retell the monologues after your model.

Later, after all the monologues have been practiced, alternate turns presenting different monologues. If you feel the child needs a reason for presenting the monologue, set the situation up as a role-playing act. Say, "Let's pretend that some community workers are coming to preschool/day care today. Each one is going to tell about his job. Let's pretend we're the community workers." Sample monologues follow or create your own. Don't be rigid in the dialogues or expect the child to remember the monologues exactly.

Firefighter: Hi. I'm a firefighter. I wear boots and a jacket to keep me dry. I wear a hat to protect my head. I use a hose to put out fires. I use a ladder to rescue people. I like to help people.

Teacher: Hi. I'm a teacher. I like to read books. I like to make pictures. I like to teach children. Sometimes we sing songs. Sometimes we have snacks.

Police Officer: Hi. I'm a police officer. I like to help people. Sometimes I catch bad guys. Sometimes I direct traffic. Sometimes I help lost kids. I have a badge and a car with a siren.

Waiter/waitress: Hi. I'm a waiter (waitress). I work in a restaurant. I bring people food to eat. I like to talk to people all day.

Doctor: Hi. I'm a doctor. I help sick people. I have a stethoscope. Sometimes I work in a hospital. I look in people's throats. I tell them to say, "ah."

Step 4, continued

Custodian: Hi. I'm a custodian. I work in a school. I help keep the school clean. I sweep floors and empty trash cans. I fix things that are broken. I like the school to look nice.

Plumber: Hi. I'm a plumber. I fix pipes. Sometimes pipes break and water goes everywhere. I know what to do. Sometimes I get wet and dirty, but I like my work. I use lots of wrenches.

Carpenter: Hi. I'm a carpenter. I like to build things. I use hammers, nails, and saws. I like to build houses.

Painter: Hi. I'm a painter. I paint houses. I use brushes, ladders, and paint. I put a big cover on the ground so I won't make a mess.

Activity 4

Materials: any Animal Puppets and Animal Monologues, Materials Book, pages 160 and 168-169, or toy animals

Home Activity: any Animal Puppets and Animal Monologues, Materials Book, pages 160 and 168-169

Directions: Show the child the toy animals or animal pictures. Introduce the activity by saying, "Today we're going to pretend we're at the farm (or zoo). The animals are going to talk to us and tell us all about themselves. First, I'll be the horse." Present a monologue from the examples below (or create your own) using easy speech. Ask the child to retell the monologue when you finish.

Then, present a second animal's monologue. If the child is fluent on the first retelling of a monologue, skip retelling the second monologue. Simply present another animal and ask the child to create an original monologue for it. If you think this will be too difficult, continue modeling and retelling the monologues following the format given above.

Later, after the child has had practice retelling all of the monologues in this way, alternate turns presenting monologues.

Lion: Hi. I'm a lion. I live in the jungle. I can roar. I can run fast. I look like a big cat.

Tiger: Hi. I'm a tiger. I live in the jungle. I have black stripes. I can run fast. I can roar like a lion.

Bear: Hi. I'm a brown bear. I live in the forest. I like to eat honey. In winter, I sleep in a cave.

Bird: Hi. I'm a robin. I live in a nest. I build my nest in a tree. I like to eat worms.

Squirrel: Hi. I'm a squirrel. I live in the forest. I like to eat nuts. I hide them in the trees.

Zebra: Hi. I'm a zebra. I live in Africa. You can see me at a zoo. I have black and white stripes. I look like a horse.

Cat: Hi. I'm a cat. I say, "Meow." I like to chase mice. I sleep a lot.

Step 4, *continued*

Dog: Hi. I'm a dog. I say, "Woof, woof." I like to chase squirrels. I like to play catch. I have a doghouse in the back yard.

Horse: Hi. I'm a horse. I say, "Neigh." I like to run in the fields. Sometimes I take people for rides on trails. I also can pull a wagon. I like to eat hay.

Pig: Hi. I'm a pig. I say, "Oink, oink." I like to roll in the mud.

Cow: Hi. I'm a cow. I say, "Moo, moo." I live in a barn. I like to eat grass. I give milk.

Duck: Hi. I'm a duck. I say, "Quack, quack." I live on a farm. I like to swim in the pond.

Penguin: Hi. I'm a penguin. I live by the ocean. I like to swim. I am black and white. I have an orange beak.

Chicken: Hi. I'm a chicken. I say, "Cluck, cluck." I live in a chicken coop. I lay eggs. I like to eat corn.

Dolphin: Hi. I'm a dolphin. I live in the ocean. I can jump out of the water. I can do flips. Sometimes I live at the zoo.

Activity 5

Materials: pictures of familiar fictional characters or toys/action figures

Home Activity: none

Directions: Have the child bring in favorite toys or dolls (e.g., dinosaurs, story characters, or action figures) or pictures of them. To ease into free play and conversation with the characters, begin by naming or describing the characters in simple sentences alternating turns. For example, say, "I see you brought in _____ today. He has a red shirt. Tell me about his hair."

Then, create a play situation with the toys or dolls where you and the child talk for the characters. Model easy speech throughout.

Step 5: Maintaining Fluency

> Goal: The child will maintain the use of easy speech during increasingly longer periods of time without direct therapeutic intervention.

The goal of this step is to phase out therapy by gradually decreasing direct contact with the child. While a progression has been presented, it's important to develop the program to meet each child's needs.

Suggestions for Support Providers

Share Home Letter #5 and/or Daycare/Preschool Letter #5 (pages 108 and 109). Maintain contact as needed.

> **Objective 1:** The child will maintain easy speech as direct therapy contacts are reduced.

Procedure

When therapy is reduced to once a week, continue Step 4 therapy. A typical session will consist of a Step 1 or 2 activity to establish fluency and then several transfer activities. If the child is disfluent, reschedule therapy to two or three times a week. Use only Step 1 and Step 2 activities until fluency is regained. Then, reintroduce Step 3 and Step 4 activities until fluency is regained before reducing therapy contacts again. If the child remains fluent, continue therapy once a week for four to six weeks. Then, reduce therapy to twice a month.

When therapy is reduced to twice a month, continue Step 4 therapy for one to two months. Encourage parents/significant others to call you with a progress report during the off weeks. A typical session will consist of a Step 1 or 2 activity to establish fluency and then several transfer activities. If stuttering begins, reschedule therapy to once a week. Use only Step 1 and Step 2 activities until fluency is regained. Then, reintroduce Step 3 and Step 4 activities until fluency is regained before reducing therapy contacts again. If the child remains fluent, continue therapy twice a month for two months. Then, reduce therapy to once a month.

When therapy is reduced to once a month, continue Step 4 therapy for two months. Encourage parents/significant others to call you with a progress report during the off weeks. You should also call the child midway between sessions. A typical session will consist of a Step 1 or 2 activity to establish fluency and then several transfer activities. If stuttering begins, reschedule therapy to twice a month or once a week. Use only Step 1 and Step 2 activities until fluency is regained. Then, reintroduce Step 3 and Step 4 activities until fluency is regained before reducing therapy contacts again. If the child remains fluent, continue seeing the child once a month for two months. Then, reduce therapy to one session in three months.

When therapy is reduced to one session in three months, continue Step 4 therapy. Have parents/significant others call you with a progress report or mail an audio or video recording of the child and family conversing at home. If the child begins to stutter, reevaluate the child. If necessary, reinstate regular therapy sessions. The frequency and nature of the therapy will be dependent on the severity of the child's stuttering. If the child remains fluent during the three-month break from therapy, dismiss the child, but arrange for a six-month recheck.

When you are only seeing the child for a six-month recheck, encourage the family to contact you if stuttering begins again.

> **Objective 2:** The child will maintain easy speech as activities provided by support personnel are reduced.

Procedure

Instruct the parents/significant others to continue to model easy speech, but to reduce the home activities to once or twice a week. If fluency is maintained, tell them to gradually decrease the activities to once a month.

When the child is maintaining fluency, and home activities are only needed occasionally, tell the parents to continue modeling easy speech but to discontinue the home activities unless it's necessary to relax the child (e.g., around holidays, birthdays, vacations, or when the child is upset, ill, or excited).

What if the child begins to stutter again based on an outside contributing factor? Is it necessary to begin therapy again immediately? It may not be necessary to resume therapy if a contributing factor has been identified and can be eliminated. It's important, however, that parents/significant others maintain contact with you on a regular schedule until fluency has been maintained for some time.

What if the child begins to stutter again, but I feel that fluency may be regained by reinstating home activities rather than therapy? It may not be necessary to resume therapy. If the parents/significant others find that resuming home activities has led to increased fluency, this may be sufficient. If stuttering continues, however, it is wise to begin therapy as soon as possible.

What if the parents expect total fluency? It's important to remind the parents/significant others that total fluency isn't the goal. Age-appropriate fluency is the goal. Talk to them again about how to distinguish normal childhood disfluencies (phrase repetitions, hesitations, revisions, whole-word repetitions of only one or two times) from stuttering (multiple whole-word repetitions, part-word repetitions, prolongations, and/or struggle behaviors). Ask the parents to contact you immediately if the child's stuttering disfluencies increase.

Combined Phonological and Fluency Therapy

Some young children will exhibit phonological disorders as well as fluency disorders. If the child you are working with falls into this category, you'll need to select a therapy strategy that targets both disorders. We have found it possible to work on both areas simultaneously, although we initially address the fluency and then gradually incorporate work on phonology. Here is a suggested outline:

I. Following a diagnostic evaluation, review the results with parents/caregivers and explain your decision to use a combined approach. Share Home Letter #6, page 110).

   A. Explain that you will begin with fluency intervention because:

      1. Fluency disorders may be harder to change and may be more socially punished later in life. Therefore, it's important to begin intervention early.

      2. Fluency progress is likely to occur quickly when intervention begins early. Therefore, the child will experience some immediate communication success and thereby become less frustrated.

      3. Since early fluency tasks involve unison, imitative, and carrier/stereotyped responses, listeners will know what the child is saying even if pronunciation is difficult to understand. Therefore, the child will experience immediate communicative success and thereby become less frustrated.

   B. Provide an explanation for the indirect/direct modeling approach you will use for fluency.

   C. Provide an explanation of the phonological therapy you will use and how it will be incorporated into the fluency program.

II. Begin fluency therapy.

   A. Initiate work on Steps 1 and 2.

      1. Begin by experiencing and establishing easy speech in therapy.

      2. Have the support providers engage in experiencing and establishing activities at home.

   B. As fluency and confidence in speaking increase in the structured tasks, gradually incorporate phonological therapy procedures.

      1. Provide the support providers with information on the phonological patterns you'll be targeting.

      2. Provide home bombardment lists.

   C. When the child has successfully completed some desensitizing and early transfer activities, begin direct phonological therapy.

      1. Alternate phonological activities with fluency activities.

      2. As fluency increases, gradually decrease fluency work and increase phonology work.

Home Letter #1

Dear Family,

I've been working on building _____'s confidence in his/her ability to speak. We've been singing songs, saying nursery rhymes, and doing finger plays. We sing and talk using slow, easy speech. The hand movements and actions are done in a slow, easy way, too.

You can help your child build confidence in speaking as well. Arrange a quiet time for you and your child. It's important that the number of people involved with quiet time be kept to a minimum. Make the time special between you and your child.

Sing or recite any of the familiar songs, nursery rhymes, and finger plays you and your child enjoy every day. Use any of those listed on the enclosed sheet or others that you and your child enjoy.

If your child doesn't know any songs, rhymes, or finger plays, tell your child that you'll do the activity twice while he/she listens. The third time, ask your child to join in. By that time, your child will probably be able to recite the key words or phrases.

If your child won't join in, suggest that he/she join when he's ready or try a different song, rhyme, or finger play. If your child continues to be unresponsive, don't demand participation. Instead, continue to spend the time together even though you're the only one participating. Eventually, your child may join you.

Enjoy the quiet time! Please call me if you have any questions.

Sincerely,

_____
Speech-Language Pathologist

_____
Phone

Daycare/Preschool Letter #1

Dear _____,

I've been trying to build _____'s confidence in his/her ability to speak by inviting him/her to sing some familiar songs and recite some familiar nursery rhymes and finger plays with me. We sing and talk using slow, easy speech. The actions are done in a slow, easy manner, too.

You can help the child build confidence in speaking as well. Arrange a quiet time during the day (5 - 10 minutes) for the two of you. It's important that the number of people involved with quiet time be kept to a minimum. Make the time special between you and the child.

Sing or recite any familiar songs, nursery rhymes, and finger plays you and your class enjoy with the child. The enclosed sheet has some suggestions.

If the child doesn't know any songs, rhymes, or finger plays, tell him/her you'll do the activity twice while he listens. The third time, ask the child to join in. By that time, the child will probably be able to recite the key words or phrases.

If the child doesn't join in, suggest that the child join when he/she is ready or try a different song, rhyme, or finger play. If the child continues to be unresponsive, instead of demanding participation, continue to engage in the tasks. Eventually, the child may join you.

Remember to sing or speak easily and slowly. The goal is for the child to participate in unison with you, not to perform the tasks for you.

Enjoy the quiet time! Please call me if you have any questions.

Sincerely,

_____
Speech-Language Pathologist

_____
Phone

Suggested Songs, Nursery Rhymes, and Finger Plays

Sing or speak the songs, rhymes, or finger plays easily and slowly.

Familiar Songs
- Old MacDonald
- London Bridge Is Falling Down
- Mary Had a Little Lamb
- Ring Around the Rosy
- Happy Birthday
- Row, Row, Row Your Boat
- Three Little Indians
- Pop Goes the Weasel
- Here We Go 'Round the Mulberry Bush
- Here We Go Looby Loo

Nursery Rhymes
- Baa, Baa, Black Sheep
- Jack and Jill
- Little Boy Blue
- Humpty Dumpty
- Hickory, Dickory, Dock
- Little Miss Muffet
- Mary, Mary, Quite Contrary
- Old King Cole
- Little Jack Horner
- Little Bo Peep

Finger Plays
- Eensy Weensy Spider
- Five Little Monkeys Jumping on a Bed
- Way Up in an Apple Tree
- I Have Two Eyes to See With
- Five Little Firemen Standing in a Row
- Here's a Church
- Six Little Ducks That I Once Knew
- I'm a Little Teapot

Home Letter #2

Dear Family,

During this step in therapy, we'll be working on modeling easy speech in structured activities. We'll begin with single words and work up to short sentences.

The first step will include imitation. I'll say a word, phrase, or sentence and ask your child to say it after me, repeating exactly what I said. Next, we'll use games in which stereotyped ("I pick a card") and carrier ("I found a _____") sentences are used. These are a little harder than imitation since there is a longer time between my model and your child's response. Also, your child has to think of one word without your model.

Then we'll add simple questions and answers to the activities. Finally, I'll encourage your child to make up original sentences about the objects or pictures in the games.

Games will be set up so your child almost always wins. I'll model "good sportsmanship" responses ("Oh, I lost and you won; Oh well, I had fun; It's fun to play even if you don't win"). I'll admit to making mistakes by saying, "Oh, look what I did. I made a mistake. Even grownups make mistakes." In these ways, I'll help your child develop positive attitudes about competition and mistakes.

Periodically, activities will be sent home so you can practice easy talking together. Try to spend 10 - 15 minutes a day in the structured play, but don't feel like you must be rigid about this. Have only one adult complete the activities with your child. Do so in a quiet place with minimal distractions or interruptions.

If your child doesn't like the activities, just work modeling of easy speech into activities like setting the table or other play times. The important thing is to have a fun time playing quietly together. Remember to speak slowly, use short sentences, pause often, and limit the number of questions you ask.

If you have questions, please feel free to call or send me a note, and I'll get back with you as soon as possible. Have a great time together!

Sincerely,

_____
Speech-Language Pathologist

_____
Phone

Daycare/Preschool Letter #2

Dear _____,

_____ is working on using slow, easy speech in structured activities and games in speech therapy. I thought you might like to know how you could incorporate the type of responses used in therapy into your classroom activities.

Basically, if you could incorporate a stereotyped or carrier sentence into a whole class activity, this would be helpful. For example, when working on colors, you might have each child respond by saying, "I see a (color + noun)" or when passing out supplies, one of the children could ask each child, "Do you need a (napkin)?" You could also have each child hold a picture of a community worker or animal and ask each other, "Who are you?" I'm sure you can think of lots of other ways to work simple sentences ("I have a _____," "I want a _____," "I need a _____," or "This is a _____") or questions into your class activities.

If you find that _____ is having a bad day, limit the amount of speech you expect and increase the opportunities for unison reciting with the whole class (e.g., songs, rhymes, whole class answers). Using songs as transitions to activities or rhymes to calm children can be effective in enhancing fluency.

You can be a good model for the child by using slow, easy speech, short sentences, and frequent pauses. When asking questions, provide choices ("Is it red or blue?") or open-ended possibilities ("How do you think we should do this?") rather than direct questions ("What do we do next?") to make responses easier for the child.

I hope this information is useful. If you have questions, feel free to contact me. I appreciate your help and feedback. What can I do in my work to help this child succeed in your setting?

Thanks for taking interest in our work.

Sincerely,

_____
Speech-Language Pathologist

_____
Phone

Home Letter #3

Dear Family,

We're now beginning work on Step 3. We'll be using easy speech during the same structured tasks used in Step 2, but now we will be adding disrupters. Certain conditions may make it harder for your child to concentrate on easy talking. To help your child resist the disruptive nature of these conditions, we'll gradually introduce them. Hopefully, your child will learn to ignore the disrupters and continue to use easy talking.

What are some of these disrupters? They vary from child to child, but include inviting people to join our sessions or having a group session from time to time. I'll also add noise such as tapping with a pencil or playing music on a tape while we play.

Sometimes we'll take our structured play activities to other locations. I may make errors in my play which will require your child to correct me and thus, help your child learn to deal with contradictions. I may interrupt your child or arrange for someone to interrupt our session. I'll also add movement to some activities. For example, your child may color or paint while imitating sentences using easy speech.

In the previous activities, I modeled easy speech and movements for your child. Now, to help your child use easy speech while under time pressures, I'll occasionally increase the rate of my speech or movements or tell your child to hurry up. Similarly, all the stories used in Step 2 were unemotional. To help your child use easy speech when talking about emotional topics like things that are happy, exciting, or scary, I'll introduce stories about these feelings.

In Step 2, I always arranged for your child to win at games in order to build confidence. Now I'll help your child learn to deal with competition by adding competitive comments and on occasion, having your child lose a game. Hopefully all of the modeling of good sportsmanship I have done in Step 2 will help your child deal with losing an occasional game.

Because I want to concentrate on situations that have disrupters, I'll contact you soon for your input. Meanwhile, continue to model easy speech at home. This is a very difficult step, so keep home activities as simple and stress-free as possible. I'll let you know when to introduce disrupters at home.

If you have questions, please feel free to call or send me a note. I'll get back to you as soon as possible. Have fun!

Sincerely,

_____
Speech-Language Pathologist

_____
Phone

Daycare/Preschool Letter #3

Dear _____,

_____ and I are now ready to begin Step 3, Desensitizing to Fluency Disrupters. We will continue to engage in structured activities, but I'll introduce elements which may be disruptive to fluency in everyday activities. Some examples include inviting other people to join the sessions or having a group session (helpful in beginning transfer to classroom situations). I'll also introduce noise such as tapping a pencil or playing music. I may arrange for interruptions such as having someone enter the room and ask me a question (also similar to classroom disruptions).

We'll engage in some activities while doing things like painting or coloring. Occasionally, we'll take our structured games to other locations. In fact, I may ask you if we can play one of our games quietly in your classroom someday. And, during some games, I'll add contradictions by making errors which _____ will have to correct.

In the past, I always modeled slow, easy speech. Now, I'll occasionally increase my rate or make comments about hurrying to add time pressures. I'll also begin to add competitive remarks and occasionally, I'll win a game. Emotional topics will also be introduced within stories used in therapy.

Because I want to practice situations which might be disruptive in the classroom, I'll talk with you soon for your input. Meanwhile, please continue to model easy speech and use unison or structured activities in the classroom as much as possible. This is a very difficult step in therapy so we need to keep outside situations (i.e., home and school) as stress-free as possible.

If you have questions, please feel free to give me a call. I really appreciate your willingness to be involved in the therapeutic process.

Sincerely,

_____
Speech-Language Pathologist

_____
Phone

Home Letter #4

Dear Family,

We're now entering Step 4 of our program. In this step, we'll work on transferring easy talking to real-life situations. This will be done by role-playing real-life situations or by using puppets to practice dialogues using easy speech.

By taking on different roles, your child will have opportunities to experiment with different pitches, rates, levels of loudness, and qualities while talking. These opportunities will help your child gain confidence in speaking. Activities will be less structured and your child will be given more opportunities to talk for longer periods of time instead of just saying one or two sentences at a time. Some free play will be included.

If you agree, we will also plan field trips to places such as the library or a fast-food restaurant to practice our easy talking. As this step begins, we'll practice both structured activities and transfer tasks. Eventually, we will spend the whole session in transfer activities.

Hopefully you are already seeing more fluency at home. If not, it should begin to be apparent as we progress through this step. Some children start to transfer spontaneously even before we begin direct work, but don't be concerned if you still hear disfluencies in conversation at home. If your child is fluent at home during the structured games, he/she is right on track. As we progress through this step, the transfer to spontaneous speech will begin to emerge.

Since this step is the hardest step, I won't be asking you to do too many new things at home at first. For now, just keep modeling easy speech in the structured activities. Remember, too, to pause often, use short sentences, and keep questions to a minimum in conversation. As your child gains success in therapy, I'll begin to send home stories and puppet plays for you and your child to do together to enhance the transfer process.

I hope you are enjoying our work as much as I am. Be sure to call if you have any questions. Also, if you have ideas for areas we should target, be sure to let me know. Your input is very important.

Sincerely,

_____
Speech-Language Pathologist

_____
Phone

Daycare/Preschool Letter #4

Dear _____,

We are now ready to begin our transfer work. In this step, we'll be working on using easy speech in real-life situations. We'll be engaging in role-playing and puppetry to practice easy talking in conversational tasks. We will also be doing some free play and going on field trips.

You may already have seen some increases in fluency in the classroom. If not, transfer should begin to occur as we progress through this step. If you have suggestions for areas we might need to target related to specific classroom activities, please let me know. Your input is very important.

Sincerely,

_____
Speech-Language Pathologist

_____
Phone

Home Letter #5

Dear Family,

Your child has made wonderful progress! It's now time to begin to "wean" your child away from the therapy routine.

To begin, we will cut back on the number of direct therapy contacts. If your child remains fluent, we'll gradually increase the time between direct contacts. As we start this process, continue your home activities on a regular basis. Then, if your child continues to maintain fluency, you can gradually reduce home practice sessions. I'll provide a schedule for how we accomplish this step.

Even though we won't be having as much direct therapy time, we need to keep in contact. Please call or drop me a note from time to time to let me know how things are going. In addition, I'll periodically call you for an update. While I don't expect any regression, be sure to contact me if you have concerns.

If your child becomes disfluent, remember to try the following. Slow your rate, pause more often, shorten your sentences, reduce the number of direct questions, use songs or rhymes for relaxation, find ways to reduce home stress, and be sure your child is getting enough rest.

I have enjoyed working with you and your child. Thanks for all your assistance.

Sincerely,

_____
Speech-Language Pathologist

_____
Phone

Daycare/Preschool Letter #5

Dear _____,

_____ has made excellent progress in our therapy program. It's now time to begin to reduce therapy contacts. I'll be setting up a maintenance schedule with the family which will involve gradually reducing the number of therapy sessions as well as reducing home practice times.

While I don't anticipate an increase in stuttering, please contact me as soon as possible should this occur. If _____ becomes disfluent, remember to use a slower rate, pause often, reduce the number of direct questions, shorten sentences, sing songs or recite rhymes for relaxation, encourage unison responses, and reduce stress and time pressures.

I'm excited about the progress we have seen. I appreciate your willingness to share in the process.

Sincerely,

_____
Speech-Language Pathologist

_____
Phone

Home Letter #6

Dear Family,

In order to help your child develop both fluent speech and age-appropriate speech sound production skills, we'll be combining fluency therapy with sound production therapy (phonological approach).

To establish fluent speech, I'll model easy speech for your child in tasks progressing from unison responses to imitative responses, carrier/stereotyped responses, questions and answers, and finally, spontaneous speech. We'll begin at the sentence level and progress into conversation. I'll send home letters describing each step of the therapy as well as suggestions for home practice.

After your child has made progress in increasing fluency, I'll begin work on sound production. At first, I'll simply have you read lists of words with the patterns for sound production we want to target so your child gets lots of practice hearing the correct patterns. It won't be necessary for your child to produce the sounds at this time.

When I think your child is ready, we'll begin working on sound production in therapy, alternating that work with the fluency work. After working on sound production in therapy, I'll send home activities for you to practice with your child.

This may seem somewhat complicated right now, but I'll keep in close contact with you so you'll know exactly what to do. If you have questions or concerns, please feel free to contact me.

Sincerely,

_____
Speech-Language Pathologist

_____
Phone

Sample Lesson Plans

Steps 1 and 2: Early Session

> Goals: The child will experience easy speech.
>
> The child will produce words, phrases, and sentences using easy speech in structured modeling tasks.

Objective	Task
1. The child will experience easy speech while singing.	singing a familiar children's song like "Old MacDonald"
2. The child will imitate words, phrases, and sentences using easy speech.	during a ball-rolling activity
3. a) The child will imitate words, phrases, and sentences using easy speech.	during an activity with a grocery basket
b) The child will produce carrier/stereotyped sentences using easy speech.	during an activity with a grocery basket
4. The child will experience easy speech while doing a finger play.	doing a familiar finger play like "Eensy Weensy Spider"

Sample Lesson Plans
Steps 1 and 2: Mid-Session

> Goals: The child will experience easy speech.
>
> The child will produce words, phrases, and sentences using easy speech in structured modeling tasks.

Objective	Task
1. The child will experience easy speech.	singing a familiar children's song like "Happy Birthday"
2. The child will imitate sentences using easy speech.	during an unemotional sequence story activity
3. a) The child will imitate words, phrases, and sentences using easy speech.	during an activity with a toy house
b) The child will produce carrier and/or stereotyped sentences using easy speech.	during an activity with a toy house
4. a) The child will imitate words, phrases, and sentences using easy speech.	during an activity with a toy zoo
b) The child will answer and/or ask questions using easy speech in structured tasks.	during an activity with a toy zoo
5. a) The child will imitate words, phrases, and sentences using easy speech.	during a picture-matching activity
b) The child will formulate sentences using easy speech in structured tasks.	during a picture-matching activity
6. The child will experience easy speech while reciting.	saying a nursery rhyme like "Jack and Jill"

Sample Lesson Plans

Steps 1 and 2: Late Session
Step 3: Early Session

> Goals: The child will experience easy speech.
>
> The child will produce words, phrases, and sentences using easy speech in structured modeling tasks.
>
> The child will produce easy speech in structured tasks in the presence of fluency disrupters.

Objective	Task
1. The child will experience easy speech while singing.	singing a familiar children's song like "Mary Had a Little Lamb"
2. a) The child will imitate words, phrases, and sentences using easy speech.	during an activity with a tool box
b) The child will answer and/or ask questions using easy speech in structured tasks.	during an activity with a tool box
3. a) The child will imitate words, phrases, and sentences using easy speech.	during a memory activity
b) The child will formulate sentences using easy speech in structured tasks.	during a memory activity
4. a) The child will imitate words, phrases, and sentences using easy speech with a parent present.	during an activity with a toy farm
b) The child will produce carrier/stereotyped sentences using easy speech with a parent present.	during an activity with a toy farm
5. a) The child will imitate sentences using easy speech with a parent present.	during an unemotional sequence story activity
b) The child will answer questions using easy speech with a parent present.	during an unemotional sequence story activity
6. The child will experience easy speech while reciting.	saying a nursery rhyme like "Hickory, Dickory, Dock"

Easy Does It For Fluency-Preschool/Primary — Copyright © 1998 LinguiSystems, Inc.

Sample Lesson Plans

Step 1: Optional
Step 2: Late Session
Step 3: Mid-Session

> Goals: The child will experience easy speech.
>
> The child will produce words, phrases, and sentences using easy speech in structured modeling tasks.
>
> The child will produce easy speech in structured tasks in the presence of fluency disrupters.

Objective	Task
1. a) The child will imitate words, phrases, and sentences using easy speech.	during a task using cleaning items
b) The child will formulate sentences using easy speech.	during a task using cleaning items
2. The child will produce carrier/stereotyped sentences using easy speech in the presence of nonverbal and verbal noise.	during a Colorform® activity with music in the background
3. The child will produce easy speech in question-and-answer tasks in the presence of contradictions.	during an activity with a school box
4. The child will imitate sentences using easy speech in the presence of emotional topics.	during an emotional sequence story activity
5. The child will produce easy speech in carrier/stereotyped sentences in the presence of verbal competitive remarks (the child wins).	during a memory activity
6. Optional: The child will experience easy speech while reciting.	reciting a familiar finger play like "Way Up in an Apple Tree"

Sample Lesson Plans

Step 1: Optional
Step 3: Late Session
Step 4: Early Session

> Goals: The child will experience easy speech.
>
> The child will produce easy speech in structured tasks in the presence of fluency disrupters.
>
> The child will use easy speech in real-life situations.

Objective	Task
1. Optional: The child will experience easy speech while singing.	singing a familiar children's song like "Row, Row, Row Your Boat"
2. a) The child will imitate sentences about an emotional topic using easy speech.	during an emotional sequence story
b) The child will answer questions about an emotional topic using easy speech.	during an emotional sequence story
3. The child will produce easy speech in carrier/stereotyped sentences in the presence of competition (the child loses).	playing a game like "Go Fish®"
4. The child will produce easy speech in carrier/stereotyped sentences in the presence of verbal competition (the child wins).	playing a picture memory game
5. The child will use easy speech in puppet play.	acting out a classroom ritual
6. Optional: The child will experience easy speech while doing actions.	doing a familiar finger play like "Five Little Firemen"

Easy Does It For Fluency-Preschool/Primary

Sample Lesson Plans

Step 1: Optional
Step 3: Late Session
Step 4: Mid-Session

> Goals: The child will experience easy speech.
>
> The child will produce easy speech in structured tasks in the presence of fluency disrupters.
>
> The child will use easy speech in real-life situations.

Objective	Task
1. The child will produce easy speech in stereotyped and/or carrier sentences in the presence of emotional topics.	using family event pictures
2. The child will use easy speech while informing.	retelling familiar stories
3. The child will use easy speech while ritualizing.	role-playing phone calls
4. The child will use easy speech while controlling.	during structured and unstructured puppet plays
5. The child will use easy speech while expressing emotions.	retelling Classroom Feeling stories
6. The child will experience easy speech while singing.	singing a familiar children's song like "Ring Around the Rosy"

Sample Lesson Plans

Step 1: Optional
Step 4: Late Session

> Goals: The child will experience easy speech.
>
> The child will use easy speech in real-life situations.

Objective	Task
1. The child will experience easy speech while reciting.	reciting a familiar nursery rhyme like "Mary, Mary, Quite Contrary"
2. The child will use easy speech while ritualizing.	role-playing ordering at a restaurant
3. The child will use easy speech while ritualizing during a field trip.	ordering at a restaurant
4. The child will use easy speech while expressing feelings.	retelling a Classroom Feeling story at a restaurant
5. The child will use easy speech while informing.	giving an account of a field trip to a parent